THE CHARACTER OF A LEADER

A Handbook for the Young Leader

DONALD ALEXANDER

In a president, character is everything. A president doesn't have to be brilliant...He doesn't have to be clever; you can hire clever...You can hire pragmatic, and you can buy and bring in policy wonks. But you can't buy courage and decency, you can't rent a strong moral sense. A president must bring those things with him...He needs to have, in that much maligned word, but a good one nonetheless, a vision of the future he wishes to create...But a vision is worth little if a president doesn't have the character—the courage and heart—to see it through.

Peggy Noonan,
columnist and author

The picture on the front cover is a representation of the Chigi vase, dating from mid-seventh-century BC Greece, now on display at the National Etruscan Museum in Rome. It contains one of the first-known paintings of a Greek hoplite phalanx.

The following examination of leadership is adapted from a set of lectures first prepared for an internal leadership course for officers preparing to deploy abroad. I wrote this book in the belief that nothing is more important for the Intelligence Community, and for the success of the nation in general, than leadership, and nothing is more important for leadership than integrity. It is being published for a wider audience, in the belief that the principles articulated here in the context of the Intelligence Community are more broadly applicable to leading across the social spectrum.

MᴄLᴇᴀɴ, Vɪʀɢɪɴɪᴀ
Aᴘʀɪʟ 2015

CONTENTS

FOREWORD

Donald Alexander is a legendary American intelligence officer. He is a man of enormous competence, grace, and courage. His humility will never allow most who cross his path to ever know what his service has meant to the Central Intelligence Agency or to our country. Now he has given us all a timeless gift—a book on leadership based on decades of experience, research, and reflection. With clear and direct language, he demystifies a subject many have written about. His emphasis on old-fashioned values and selfless, compassionate service should be mandatory reading for anyone entrusted with the care and development of young men and women, whether in government or a Silicon Valley start-up. This is a book that will challenge and inspire you to make a difference every day of your life. It may be Donald Alexander's greatest service to us all.

George J. Tenet
Former Director of Central Intelligence

Extraordinarily effective and innovative professional leadership is the most important ingredient in the initial and continuous success of any organization or activity, whether in military, government, industry, a small business, or even a family. Donald Alexander has had a driving and compelling interest in the critical topic of "leadership" for many years, and perhaps more importantly, he has also demonstrated the continuous, wildly successful application of leadership broadly in his own professional life, so he knows whereof he speaks. He has also demonstrated outreach on leadership issues with other organizations and has electrified these organizations with his own ideas and passion on the importance of leadership, especially the importance of character and integrity.

I have been a professional in the military, in the Intelligence Community, in government, and in industry for over fifty years. I have observed the preeminent power of "leadership with integrity" and the downside of poor leadership. It is undoubtedly the most important ingredient for organizational success, bar none. In this book, Alexander has captured the complexity, essence, attributes, and importance of effective leadership. His use of history, his organization of great leadership attributes, and his commentary on implementation of leadership in case after case make the points about the unparalleled preeminence and effectiveness of strong leadership and about what skills are required to wield the strong leadership that makes it all work.

In my career, both in the Navy and the Intelligence Community, I have been associated with true renaissance and game-changing activities that were truly historic (and yet to be fully declassified). In all these cases, strong, confident, competent, and unrelenting leadership carried the day. In all cases, they produced eye-watering intelligence critical to our national security, informing policy, neutralizing terrorist operations, heading off wars. The author of this book has captured all the factors that would apply in these successful cases.

We all owe Donald Alexander a debt of gratitude for his devoted study and recounting of this important topic, and also for his highly readable and articulate explication of a difficult subject. I commend this book to all concerned, especially if you are serious about making a true difference in the complex and dangerous world.

Bill Studeman
Admiral, US Navy, Ret.
Former Director, National Security Agency
Former Deputy Director of Central Intelligence

When I met this humble man of character, it was immediately apparent that he has a passion and talent for conveying leadership best practices to all who would listen…and all did. It was after this rewarding encounter that I discovered he had written this book, and I immediately purchased and read it. It is a quick, fun read, but it's now a dog-eared, yellow-highlighted "leadership reference book" with notes in the margins that I carry with me to every leadership class or presentation. There are hundreds, if not thousands, of books written on leadership, but Donald Alexander has found a way to operationalize the theory and to provide leadership tools that work from the battlefield to the boardroom and in our personal lives.

Every commander must have a command (leadership) philosophy that sets the atmosphere for the daily functioning of the unit. The same applies in business or any other walk of life. Leaders must keep it simple, say it often, and live it daily. *The Character of a Leader* provides the framework for creating a selfless/servant atmosphere that will inspire loyalty, demand integrity, and energize all to commit to the cause and achieve results.

A motivating quick read, this book is a must for young, aspiring leaders and a great course check for the senior/midlevel executive.

John F. Sattler
LtGen United States Marine Corps, Ret.

DEDICATION

With all my heart, to Donald and Alexander, who made us immensely proud and who, early on, far surpassed their father in leadership, character, and courage.

INTRODUCTION

The market today is flooded with treatises on leadership in all its variations, perspectives, and applications. Ironically, while discussions on leadership are very much in vogue, there is everywhere in the country evidence that this attention has not led to an overabundance of quality leaders. How does one write something original on the subject? How does one write something comprehensive on such an immense, important, and multifaceted subject? How is this book different? What original does it bring to the discussion? And to what particular audience is it directed?

In college, I was a member of the Naval Reserve Officer Training Corps/Marine Option, where I aspired to become a Marine officer, a leader of men, one of "The Few, the Proud." As most people know, nothing in the Marine Corps is more important than leadership, and of course I wondered if I would develop into a capable leader. To my lasting regret, an injury at the US Army Airborne School at Fort Benning uncovered a congenital medical defect that, while not serious, was enough to put me on the fast track to a medical discharge. I felt lost and wondered what I would do with my life that would approach the Marine Corps for that feeling of meaningful service. Searching for something that might come close to that challenge, I applied to the Central Intelligence Agency. There must have been a critical shortage of applicants that year since, despite my rather unimpressive college record, I found myself walking through the front door of that institution in November 1967 as a Professional Trainee. (Despite the impressive-sounding title, I spent the next two years and three months in the basement of Headquarters, cleaning out dusty old files and indexing names in the records division.)

Now, forty-seven years later, I look back on my career, having joined the ranks of those who understand that, like the Marine Corps, the CIA and every other organization with any kind of challenging mission succeeds or fails very much on the quality of its leaders. The following observations, then, represent reflections on almost five decades of service in the US Intelligence Community (IC) where I've served in the senior ranks as an operations officer and program manager, both in the field and at Headquarters. They are not borne of any formal "management training." They are, instead, the product of lessons from my own family, which has spawned some remarkable leaders, and experience on the job, where I have had the privilege of serving with leaders of exceptional quality—men and women of character, vision, and ability; men and women who embody the values I will describe; men and women who have served their country with great honor, courage, and selflessness. The nation will never fully know what it owes to these quiet heroes.

The approach to leadership in this book may strike some as overly elementary. I have given presentations along these lines to groups of officers of all ranks and frequently find that some—particularly the more senior ones—take umbrage at the implication that they might lack the qualities described here. After all, why else would they have been elevated to the senior ranks? On the other hand, there have been times in my career when the workforce has had some pretty hard words for these selfsame leaders. These experiences have led me to target this book at the young man or woman starting out on a career and facing those same questions and trepidations I faced so many years ago: What exactly is this esoteric thing called "leadership"? Will I measure up? Where and how am I to learn this skill? What if I can't figure it out?

Leadership, like a lot of other disciplines, often comes cloaked in arcane academese or sociological babble, seemingly as remote and unattainable to the unwashed as String Theory in physics. Recently I learned a new acronym as documents have passed my desk (actually, they no longer pass my desk; they pass my computer screen, but I still hearken back to my paper days in the old Records and Files Division)—that term is BLUF, which stands for "bottom line up front." My BLUF to young, aspiring leaders is that the basic metaphysical framework of leadership is quite simple and straightforward. It's like running a triathlon: you swim so far, bike so far, and then run—pretty simple in concept, but it takes a lot of hard work, dedication, and discipline to do it effectively. So it is with leadership. Be a person of integrity, put your mission and people before yourself; conduct yourself with honor. It's that simple—in concept—but it takes continuous effort and discipline to get there.

While my own experience in leadership has been almost entirely within the Intelligence Community, and many of the examples and quotes herein come from the intelligence/military world, I believe that these principles are universal. Take the situations and examples given and translate them into *your* world; I think you'll find they fit well.

I can claim no received wisdom on this subject and, given the vast body of relevant scholarship out there, it would be presumptuous to claim much originality. Nor could these ideas lay claim to being comprehensive, leadership being a subject of almost infinite dimension, complexity, and variety. The literature on the broad range of skills it takes to be a great leader would fill many bookshelves, if not a complete library; I'm sure there were cubbyholes filled with scrolls on the subject in the library at Alexandria in ancient Egypt. Aspiring leaders hunger to know if the great leader needs to be charismatic, or tenacious, or empathetic. Where to find the answers?

Leadership has been subjected to much "academic" research. If you read the studies, you find that Neuroscientist A conducted a study that concluded X. His critics vociferously disagree, citing flaws in methodology, sampling size, etc. Professor B conducted another study that concluded Y—and his critics just as quickly tear at his findings. Businessman C draws on his years as CEO to point to the "essential elements of leadership." Professor D charges that Businessman C couldn't manage a Burger King. (Businessman C promptly sues Professor D.) It's a bit like a mix of positively and negatively charged particles—you shake the bag, the particles bang together, and…you're literally back at zero. So, what does all this investigation tell us, this continuing battle of studies—with their consequent checklists of principles, traits, and habits—that seems destined to go on forever with no resolution in sight? Again, the studies are all over the place. Moreover, you are who you are, and you simply aren't going to rewire your personality that much.

So what's an aspiring leader to do? Cheerfully conceding up front that I will be adding another to this endless list of traits, prescriptions, and formulas, I will argue that leadership lies not in a recipe—"follow this list and be a great leader"—but a methodology for studying your task and developing your own bespoke style of leadership, custom tailored to you, all necessarily constructed on a solid foundation of character and values.

You take some of what I would call the anchor principles (integrity, etc.), learn to assess your mission and situation, and then craft yourself into the best leader you can be in the given situation. Don't worry about the formulas and whether you measure up; it's like saying "blondes have more fun": great if you're a blonde, but what if you're a redhead? Leaders come in all shapes, sizes, and personalities. In his well-reviewed study of the senior admirals who led the US Navy in the Second World War, Walter Borneman writes of William Leahy, the chairman of the Joint Chiefs of Staff; Ernest King, Chief of Naval Operations; Chester Nimitz, Commander-in-Chief, Pacific Fleet; and William "Bull" Halsey, Commander of the 3rd and 5th Fleets. Borneman quotes Vice Admiral Roland Smoot as remarking,

> *I've tried to analyze the four five-star admirals that we've had in this Navy…You have a man like King—a terrifically "hew the line" hard martinet, stony steely gentleman; the grandfather and really lovable old man Nimitz—the most beloved man I've ever known; the complete clown Halsey—a clown but if he said "Let's go to hell together" you'd go to hell with him; and then the diplomat Leahy— the open-handed, effluent diplomat Leahy. Four more different men never lived, and they all got to be five-star admirals.*

(What's more, they enjoyed a fierce rivalry and didn't seem to be too fond of each other either.) According to Borneman, Smoot answered his own question with one word: *leadership.* They all had

> *the ability to make men admire them one way or the other, King by bluster and verve; Nimitz by putting his hand on your shoulder and saying, Let's get this thing done; Halsey—still the fullback—by rushing through the line in such a way that everyone on the team wanted to go through with him; and Leahy by never letting his own personal feelings, or those of others, interfere with the long-range objectives and best interests of his country.*[1]

In early 2013, professing himself "disturbed" in the wake of widely publicized misconduct on the part of an alarming number of serving senior military officers, Chairman of the Joint Chiefs of Staff General Martin Dempsey felt compelled to reinforce his insistence on ethical behavior and instituted a number of measures to get a better assessment of the performance—and particularly the personal character—of his senior officers. "You can have someone of incredible character who can't lead their way out of a forward operating base because they don't have the competence to understand the application of military power, and that doesn't do me any good," General Dempsey said. "Conversely, you can have someone who is intensely competent, who is steeped in the skills of the profession, but doesn't live a life of character. And that doesn't do me any good."[2]

The problem is certainly not limited to the military. The once-vaunted US Secret Service has experienced its own series of leadership crises in recent years, as described in an op-ed piece in *The Washington Post* by retired Secret Service agent Dan Emmett:

1 Walter Borneman, *The Admirals: Nimitz, Halsey, Leahy, and King—The Five-Star Admirals Who Won the War at Sea* (New York: Little, Brown, 2012).

2 Thom Shanker, "Conduct at Issue as Subordinates Review Officers," *New York Times*, April 14, 2013.

There are too many incompetent managers who want the title, pay and perks of management while performing no duties of leadership.... Even the best units perform poorly with poor leaders.... If managers show continued lapses in judgment, how and why would anyone expect the rank and file to behave better?...When I became a Secret Service agent in 1983, most of our top and mid-level supervisors were armed forces veterans; they managed and led by the ethos of military leadership, which dictates accomplishing the mission while taking care of those entrusted to them. They expected much from their subordinates but knew that they must set the example we would follow.... The Secret Service of today is awash in managers, not leaders. Many supervisors have little tangible or leadership experience, yet they are designated as managers on the basis of their titles and long lists of schools attended.... Alas, leadership cannot be taught in a classroom alone. In the military, people must first pass Officer Candidate School before assuming leadership roles. In the federal government, more often than not, people are promoted first and then trained as leaders— the concept is entirely backward...The Secret Service should begin a leadership school for entry-level managers, preferably conducted by the military. While major corporations and the federal government have become huge proponents of every type of management and business school imaginable, and have spent millions of dollars sending their neophyte managers to them, the military best understands leadership in its most basic form.... It is the commander who bears the ultimate responsibility for subordinates' actions.[3]

---

3 Dan Emmett, "Alcohol Isn't the Secret Service's Problem. Lousy Leadership Is," *Washington Post*, March 28, 2014. http://www.washingtonpost.com/opinions/alcohol-isnt-the-secret-services-problem-lousy-leadership-is/2014/03/28/6cc1b48c-b5be-11e3-b899-20667de76985_story.html.

In the end, all the checklists and handbooks can only provide building blocks for what must become a custom-built leadership style that you must in the end craft from your own personality, your own experience, your own character, and the particular challenges of your work. Make the best of the strengths God gave you. What you will find here can only represent a *start*—not the be-all-and-end-all—of an examination of the broader spectrum of leadership. Some of my observations may strike the reader as obvious. But if they were so obvious, authors would not continue to feed their families and put their kids through college on the proceeds of leadership handbooks that would-be leaders so avidly gobble up. Obvious or not, in the end, I can only hope this work will be of some utility to the reader.

One of my two central themes in this book will be that in leadership, *character counts*. First, in the substantive sense, all other things being equal, a person of strong character will be a more effective leader than someone of deficient character (effectiveness being the overall, bottom-line measure of performance against goals). The ancient Greek philosopher Heraclitus of Ephesus said this all the way back in the fifth century BC, and even then he probably wasn't the first to make the connection: *ethos anthropos daimon*, which can be translated as "a man's character is his fate."

No less a man than Ernest Shackleton, leader of the 1914–1917 British Imperial Trans-Antarctic Expedition, believed that character and temperament were as important as technical skills.[4] He well understood that, as a leader, your behavior is constantly being observed and evaluated by your seniors, your peers, and your team. Your ability to "lead" them will, therefore, be *directly proportional to their trust in you*, which is in turn a product of character, integrity, and professional competence.

The second important theme, closely related to the above, is that *effective leadership is necessarily predicated on the consent of the led.*

---

4 Roland Huntford, *Shackleton* (London: Hodder & Stoughton, 1985).

While you can be appointed to a position of leadership, it is your team that confers on you the honor of the title "leader." You're much more likely to take it across the goal line if they have confidence in your integrity, matched, of course, with professional competence and the ability to successfully conceive and implement a successful strategy.

To our great detriment, Americans these days find it difficult to have a reasonable dialogue about values, and what talk there is seems to devolve into a disappointingly raucous, uncivil, and unproductive shouting match. On the one hand, those who most personify these values tend by nature to be reticent in discussing things like honor, courage, and patriotism. Our parents raised us to know the difference because they had learned it from their parents, and it was a societal consensus. That societal consensus was built on an evolution of our thinking—from the ages of barbarism through feudalism, and then to the Enlightenment, that came to see that values like integrity and selflessness were the best guideposts to a more just, peaceful, and productive society.

On the other side of the line of scrimmage are the cynics and postmodernists—moral relativists who tell us that morals are just a matter of individual determination and that values are the last refuge of dead, white, male scoundrels. These "non-judgmentalists" demand to know by what right we presume to stand in judgment over others. They find a high regard for values distasteful at the least, if not downright discriminatory, elitist, even illegal. It used to be that we were pretty good at labeling things good or evil, true or false. Modern "progressivism" argues that "values" judgments do not reflect objective reality or a moral absolute, but only an assertion of the speaker's personal perspective. Everyone is entitled to his own interpretation of "the facts."

In an article entitled "Where the Wild Things Are," *New York Times* columnist David Brooks writes about two different perspectives on morality and character. Brooks refers to Princeton philosopher Kwame Anthony Appiah's book *Experiments in Ethics*, wherein Appiah contrasts the philosopher's view of morality with the psychologist's: the philosopher holds that "each of us has certain ingrained character traits.

An honest person will be honest most of the time." Some psychologists, on the other hand, would claim that their research proves that individuals don't have one thing called character:

[P]eople's actual behavior is not driven by permanent traits... People don't have one permanent thing called character. We each have a multiplicity of tendencies inside, which are activated by this or that context.... In the philosopher's picture, the good life is won through direct assault. Heroes use reason to separate virtue from vice. Then they use willpower to conquer weakness, fear, selfishness and the dark passions lurking inside.... In the psychologist's version, the good life is won indirectly. People have only vague intuitions about the instincts and impulses that have been implanted in them by evolution, culture and upbringing.[5]

Smarter men than I have marshaled a wide spectrum of argument against this moral relativism. The Irish author C. S. Lewis, perhaps best known for his works on Christian philosophy, published *The Abolition of Man*, originally a series of lectures on education at the University of Durham. In it, he argues for the Tao, a term he coined to represent the traditional moralities of East and West[6] that he "lumped together" for his rhetorical purpose, a value system that believes in right and wrong, good and evil, and has no problem differentiating between the two, this as opposed to moral and ethical relativism that are even more prevalent in our day than they were in Lewis' (as he, in fact, predicted). He believes in the doctrine of objective value, the belief that certain attitudes are true and others are false. His major point is that if we continue to debunk and devalue our traditional institutions and values, it will result in the "abolition of man," the dehumanization of society. (Lewis was

---

5 David Brooks, "Where the Wild Things Are," *New York Times*, October 20, 2009.

6 In this, Lewis is drawing from the major religious traditions of East and West, but is specifically making the point that he is *not* basing his arguments on religion per se or arguing for his reader to accept it, but on the societal and moral values common to them.

writing this in dark days of the Second World War.) He noted that education was a kind of propagation of society's shared values to each new generation, but that in recent years (and even more so in our current time) education runs more to propaganda of the relativist view. Lewis contends that, without firm moral foundations, there is no framework on which to base our decisions, behaviors, and judgments. We are thus cast adrift of our ethical moorings, with predictable results. He writes, "The head (intellect) rules the belly (appetites) through the chest—the seat of...emotions organized by trained habit into stable sentiments." The "chest" stands for those values and moral disciplines that protect us from blindly following our basest instincts.

The Chest...Sentiment—these are the indispensible liaison officers between cerebral man and visceral man. It may even be said that it is by this middle element that man is man; for by his intellect he is mere spirit and by his appetite he is mere animal.

The operation of [moral relativism]...is to produce what may be called Men without Chests. It is an outrage that they should be commonly spoken of as Intellectuals.... Their heads are no bigger than the ordinary: it is the atrophy of the chest beneath that makes them seem so...

We make men without chests and expect from them virtue.... We laugh at honor and are shocked to find traitors in our midst.... Without the aid of trained emotions [the chest], the intellect [head] is powerless against the animal organism [the belly]...

This thing which I have called for convenience the Tao, and which others may call Natural Law or Traditional Morality...is not one among a series of possible systems of value. It is the sole source of all value judgments. If it is rejected, all value is rejected...What purport to be new systems or (as they now call them) "Ideologies," all consist of fragments from the Tao itself.[7]

These principles are every bit as applicable, if not more, to leadership as they are to other aspects of society. True societal or personal ethics are only possible within the framework of a rigorous, consistent, and clear set of moral standards and values. Character and integrity are the multi-axis gyroscopic navigation system that keeps us on our moral course. Remove that and we are free-floating through the moral universe, untethered and unable to reach our destination of life, liberty, and the pursuit of happiness.

Many will argue against my central regard for character, and they are welcome to their point of view. It's a debate very much worth having, and I will attempt to present my case in the following pages. But I know where the people I admire most fall on the scale of character versus a "multiplicity of tendencies," willpower versus "vague intuitions." Give me every time the guy or gal who uses—or at least strives to use, albeit imperfectly and not with universal success—"willpower to conquer weakness, fear, selfishness and the dark passions lurking inside"[8]. In short, I remain unshakeable in my belief that effective, long-term leadership must be based on a rock-solid foundation of moral values. A real leader is first and foremost a person of professional and personal integrity. Otherwise, looking at it from the most basely parochial perspective, why would any follower in his right mind willingly place his occupational future—to say nothing of his life—in the care of a untrustworthy "leader," who lied and who put his interests over those of his charges? And why would any senior executive in his or her right mind entrust an important mission to such a "leader"? No "vague intuitions and impulses" can excuse abandoning the phalanx once the shield walls have collided.

---

7 C. S. Lewis, *The Abolition of Man* (Las Vegas: Lits, 2010): 19.

8 Brooks, "Where the Wild Things Are," *New York Times*.

It is unarguable that you will find people in positions of leadership who fall dishearteningly short in this measure. I would only say that, in my book, they are not "leaders" in the true sense of the word. I believe this is a distinction with a difference, and I believe that in the long term, leaders of integrity have the best chance of achieving success and preserving the values that are most important to us as Americans, values that have been at the root of our nation's liberty and prosperity these last two centuries. The more intractable the task, the more complex the issues, the more risky the undertaking—all the more important is it that the troops be able to take the leader at his or her word and have confidence that the leader's decisions and strategies are motivated by mission accomplishment, not self-promotion and self-aggrandizement.

In these pages, I'll be citing a number of books and articles to which the reader may wish to refer. I made the point earlier that the market today is flooded with books that purport to instruct in leadership. For those wishing to delve more deeply into this vital subject, though, there is one I would particularly like to recommend: *Leadership: The Warrior's Art*, a comprehensive anthology of essays on leadership written and edited by Christopher Kolenda when he was on the faculty of the history department at West Point. While the contributors were all serving or retired military professionals, these pieces are by no means less applicable to leadership in other fields of endeavor. Kolenda, a veteran of three tours with the US Army in Afghanistan, himself wrote the kick-off essay, one of the better examinations I have encountered of what leadership is, providing a historical perspective going back to classical Greece and Rome. He writes of Socrates, Plato, Aristotle, and Xenophon (this last a pupil of Socrates and a professional soldier who wrote *Anabasis*, a firsthand account of the orderly retreat of a stranded Greek army—the legendary "Ten Thousand"—from the depths of the Persian Empire in about 400 BC). Citing the Roman philosopher Cicero on the subject of the importance of integrity and character in leadership, Kolenda writes that:

Critical to building the inner substance of trustworthiness for these ancient philosophers was the notion of sophrosyne (moderation). Sophrosyne means the wisdom of self-mastery and self-discipline, what Cicero calls "the science of doing the right thing at the right time." According to Neal Wood, the Socratic principle of self-discipline is central to Xenophon's conception of leadership.[9] For Xenophon, those who lack self discipline are absolutely slavish, and no "slave" to money, luxury, glory, sex, etc. could become a trustworthy leader. Slavishness showed a lack of courage, the inability to discipline the desires, and thus an absence of the inner strength to choose right from wrong.... People who cannot control their desires, these ancients argue, will erode the fabric of the relationship between leader and led and are thus unfit to lead. Those with good character, on the other hand, draw others toward them and uplift them. The pursuit of excellence demands both character and competence.[10]

Kolenda accepts that there is another side to this argument about the central importance of leadership, though he acknowledges that it's probably one of those metaphysical debates neither side can win. That said, I'm squarely on the side of the ancients and will attempt to lay out my arguments in the following pages. In the meantime, *The Warrior's Art* is a valuable resource for the aspiring leader and well worth reading for anyone who wants to immerse him or herself deeply in the history and philosophy of leadership.

Character by itself, of course, is no guarantee of success as a leader. And it would be hard to prove in any systematic way that you can't sometimes get good results from bad leaders. It's an unfortunate fact that many people who are fueled chiefly by ambition and ego make it

---

9 Neal Wood, "Xenophon's Theory of Leadership," *Classica et Mediaevalia* 25 (1964): 33–66.

10 Christopher D. Kolenda, "What Is Leadership? Some Classical Ideas," in *Leadership: The Warrior's Art* (Carlisle, PA: Army War College Foundations Press, 2001): 17-23.

to the top, often outnumbering the more honorable. These people rise by clawing their way past their peers while ingratiating themselves by kissing up to their clueless senior managers. Promoted to "leadership," they rule through intimidation and fear, employing bullying and public humiliation to demonstrate their power. I spoke recently with a friend who is a senior officer in another government agency, and he ticked off a long list of disagreeable characters, narcissists, and general misanthropes who currently occupy senior positions there. One is infamous for screaming at her workforce. Another will stab any back that makes the mistake of passing within dagger range. I once personally observed a (world-famous) cabinet secretary tear into a GS-4 (entry-level) secretary, just out of her teens, simply because his lunch was carried into the room by the wrong person at the wrong time. In my book, no amount of policy genius can excuse that kind of brutish behavior. No one I knew wanted to be within a mile of him, aside from the school of remoras, already his equal in despicability, glued tightly to his underbelly in their desperate hunger for scraps of attention and proximity to celebrity.

Why are these foul people brought into the organization, tolerated, and promoted to positions of leadership? Why are they so often in the majority despite their being hated and feared? In many cases, it's not even that they are outstanding performers who just happen to be nasty SOBs; it's not at all uncommon to see people at the top who are loathsome *and* incompetent. Why is that? Why doesn't natural selection remove from the professional gene pool these deplorable leaders, who drag down morale and performance, and whom people follow only out of fear or lack of the means of escape? I must admit I can't explain it. I can only say again that, in my experience, people respond better, work harder, and produce better results for a leader of character. Think of the great leaders of history, like Washington, Lincoln, and Churchill, men—while, like all of us, imperfect—of unshakable character and integrity. Then think of the dissembling, self-absorbed, machine politicians of today and decide who you want to model yourself after.

The Romans of the (pre-imperial) Republic—*res publica*, literally "the thing of the people"—understood that freedom can only flourish if energized by civic virtue. Without this common set of values, shared both among citizens and their leaders, the very mortar that binds the brickwork of society can quickly crumble. This applies equally to both organizations and institutions. The United States Marine Corps, an organization that understands the critical importance of integrity and is not ashamed to talk about it, has a lot to teach us about imbuing an enterprise with the values that forge a diverse group into a cohesive, productive, victorious team. If you want to read some compelling disquisitions on the importance of values, search out the speeches of former US Marine Commandant General Charles Krulak.[11] You will find him one of the most thoughtful and articulate writers on leadership and integrity in recent times. As a society, we need to shed this discomfort with discussing foundational values and, like General Krulak, make them the subject of regular, rigorous, and open discussion.

There are those who balk simply at the whole idea of leadership. They imagine the organization chart as one broad, horizontal rank of equals. A college professor recently enlightened me on this subject, describing a post-modern culture drilled into her students that cautions against doing anything to stand out or in any way imply that they are "better" than their peers or have any right to "boss them around." Hard as it may be to believe, readings in her field often characterize leadership as a negative, a power held by one over another. To this way of thinking, if someone leads, someone must be the follower and somehow thereby inferior, which might hurt his or her self-esteem. (I guess when the stakes are not high, you can afford such affectations.) And since no one is perfect, no one, they maintain, has any business being "judgmental" about others or telling them how they should behave. This delusional philosophy comes to us from the 1960s generation of "do

---

11 For example, see his keynote speech to the Joint Services Conference on Professional Ethics (JSCOPE) in January 2000, available at http://www.appleseeds.org/krulak_integrity.htm.

your own thing" and "cool it, prof; course grades are so fifties," or "the text means what I, the reader, choose to say it does." Among the many problems with that world view is that if no one can judge anyone else, then there are no standards and no publicly agreed-on mores to keep us all on the right side of civilized behavior. That way lies the sure road to the breakdown of civilization and a return to barbarism. I suggested to the professor that she ask her students to consider two different problem sets, one tactical and one strategic, in order to appreciate the practical need for leadership in the real world.

First, the tactical. Think back to New York City on September 11. Chaos reigned as people literally jumped from the windows of upper floors of the Twin Towers to avoid the flames. Hundreds of firemen, policemen, and first responders from a myriad of organizations and departments quickly converged on the scene. These individuals, along with scores of those working in the buildings, showed unimaginable courage, many paying with their lives as the buildings collapsed. Individuals working independently would have been overwhelmed; it could not have worked without leadership. That so many were saved was the result of leadership by (and courage of) New York public safety officials orchestrating who went where and took on what tasks. What was needed was...a leader—someone to quickly assess the situation and develop a plan of action. "Take your men and hook up the hoses; you two put the ladder up over there; you, follow me into the building." They didn't have the luxury of time to sit around a conference table, debating options, trying to reach a consensus; no time for appointing a commission to study the problem. On that day, leadership literally meant the difference between life and death.

On the strategic front, a company might be losing market share, with its stock slumping and shareholders up in arms. An immediate course correction is required. There are different departments with different responsibilities—manufacturing, marketing, and advertising—each with its own different (often conflicting) set of equities and priorities. A new CEO is brought in by the board of directors to turn the company around. With advice from the board and her management team, she must plot a new course to resuscitate the company. She will get plenty of advice from all over the map: sell off this division, increase direct marketing, even the dreaded word "downsizing." (The new, more politically correct term for axing workers is "rightsizing.") The CEO must quickly come up with a vision—a road map for recovery that integrates and balances all the different equities and circumstances across the enterprise and sets the optimal course back to fiscal health. She must then convince the board of directors of the wisdom of this strategic plan and get "buy-in" from the troops, not for the day-to-day management of the previous CEO's strategy, but for a bold new direction, founded on systematic analysis and a clear vision, backed up by the rhetorical skill to build consensus and the perseverance to drive to victory. *That* is why a leader is required.

In contrast to our reticence to unabashedly address the subject of values, leadership today is at the other end of the spectrum. Legions of "authorities" have spilled oceans of ink on the topic. These examinations range from the useful to the superficial, too often rife with incomprehensible academic jargon. Yet, for being one of the most widely written about and universally studied areas of human social practice, it is surprising how unhelpful most of these discussions are. For that reason, I'd like to pose a series of fundamental questions that I hope will help you think more clearly about the subject, including such questions as: What is a leader? Why do we need leaders? What is the function of a leader? What are people looking for in a leader? What are the elements of leadership? What constitutes the character of a leader? What are the traits of a leader? How does one become a leader? And, very importantly, are leaders born or made?

A couple of general points before we get into the details:

- There are many different kinds of leadership and equally as many different ideas about teaching it. The terms "leader" and "leadership" are broad usages, with many different denotations, connotations, and contexts. There are today thousands of leadership theories and books, thousands of checklists, thousands of commentaries on the right qualities—the right stuff—needed to be a leader. There are endless lists of traits and formulas for leadership. What follows are *my* opinions, geared to *my* experience. By no means would I claim they exhaust the subject. I would suggest, though, that I believe these principles are pretty universal and will apply to almost any form of organization.

- It will be important for you to think about leadership from two perspectives—that of your superiors and what they're looking for in you as a leader, and that of those you would lead. Think about what it would take in a leader for you to unflinchingly follow him or her through the gates of hell. Think about how you want to come across to those who look to you for leadership. You'll be doing both in your career.

- It is also important to understand that the behaviors I am talking about are ideals to which we all might aspire, not hard-and-fast rules, the disobedience of which will forever disqualify you from a position of leadership. In our society today, as soon as you start talking about old-fashioned stuff like character, virtue, and values, you are subject to attack: "Who are you to question my character or lecture me about values?" Let me stop that right here. Whatever you may know of me or think of me, however imperfect you may consider me, don't get hung up on that. Don't get hung up on my flaws and who am I to talk to you about leadership. If you do, you'll never be able to discuss this with anyone, all of us being flawed mortals. That's a cop-out and a dead end. This is not about me; this is about you, the people you work for, and the people you lead. Focus on the ideas presented and let them stand or fall on the strength of their logic.

- Many recalcitrants will try to bully you by asserting that since you're not perfect, you have no right to "preach" to others, and this tactic is too often effective in silencing proponents of standards and values. This happens frequently to politicians who try to promote values. The opposition "research" wing digs for any and all imperfections in the challenger's past and then raises the cry of hypocrisy, distracting the voters' attention from the substantive issue to the red herring of the opponent's past indiscretions. Regrettably, this is often sufficient to silence those trying to promote values. Of course, none of us mere mortals can top the scale across the full spectrum of leadership qualities all the time. But you can't hide behind the dodge that since no one is perfect, there's no use even trying. What's important is to accept the premise that character and integrity are paramount and to commit to trying to achieve them. As Robert Browning so beautifully wrote, "Ah, but a man's grasp should exceed his reach, Or what's a heaven for?" It takes constant work and the realization that, while you will never achieve perfection, it's a goal worth shooting for. The alternative is the abandonment of even an attempt at character or standards—every man for himself, which can only lead to chaos and ineffectiveness.

- Keep in mind that leaders aren't just at the stratospheric level of organizations; you can lead—and make a difference—at virtually any level of an organization.

- This book is not intended to be prescriptive; rather, its purpose is to get you to personally reflect on some of the behaviors I believe are conducive to good and effective leadership and to hold them up against your own experience. From that point on, it's up to you.

- To help you think about the points I'll be raising, it might be useful for you to pick out a few people in your life you really respected as leaders and a few you did not. Keep these examples in mind as we go through this discussion.

- And finally, are leaders born or made? Like most people, throughout my career I have wondered about this in regard to my own capabilities and potential. You worry, if leaders are born, what if I didn't happen to be blessed with the magic DNA? Am I just out of luck? Is there no way I can develop into a leader? On the other hand, if leaders are made, then in what crucible—and by whom—am I to be forged? Later on, having defined what leaders and leadership are, along with the character and traits of a leader, I'll offer some thoughts on this age-old question.

Chapter 1

WHAT IS LEADERSHIP?

Management is efficiency in climbing the ladder of success; leadership determines whether the ladder is leaning against the right wall.

Stephen R. Covey,
noted author on leadership and management

MANAGEMENT vs. LEADERSHIP

Before we get into examining leaders and leadership, let's take a minute to deal with the important question of the difference between "management" and "leadership," terms often conflated. Here are some teaser quotes from prominent CEOs, taken from *The Wall Street Journal*'s website presenting an article that offers to provide "step-by-step how-tos for being a better leader":

1

[The company] holds all-night experimental coding sessions called "hackathons" to encourage employee innovation.
A meeting is not a loose opportunity to chat...
Organizations thrive when employees feel they can speak honestly.

I don't want to be unfair to these obviously highly capable and successful business leaders or to the superb *Journal*, but these are their words: All-night experimental coding sessions? Meetings are not an opportunity to chat? Organizations thrive when employees feel they can speak honestly? Of all the phrases descriptive of leadership, do these really strike you as the "essence" of leadership? Do they represent a "step-by-step guide"? Or do these statements, while admittedly material, more correctly relate to issues of management...important, but down a few levels from strategic leadership?

One way to look at leadership, as opposed to management, is that the former sets out the vision (more on this later) while the latter concerns the mechanics and logistics of implementing that vision. This is not to diminish the importance of sound management—without it, missions don't get accomplished. And, admittedly, there is a good deal of overlap—functions that straddle the border between leadership and management. In some situations, you will start out as a manager and only later be asked to step up to serious leadership. And you will often be a leader and a manager at the same time.

Leadership books are always talking about "managing change," as if change were some external, inexorable force like a wild tiger whose back you're clinging to for dear life. How about managing change in terms of being the "agent" of change—being proactive, rather than reactive? Isn't leadership, per se, more involved in the inspiration, the motivation, the psychological "conditioning" of the team to bring out their best (the whole of a well-led team's efforts being greater than the sum of its individual members' skills)? And, importantly, holding them steady in the face of adversity, unexpected setbacks, and other discouragements. (If it were easy, why would we need good leaders?) It is these defining aspects and qualities of leadership that we will be exploring below.

WHAT IS A LEADER?

All truths are easy to understand once they are discovered. The point is to discover them.

Galileo

Leadership is widely held to be one of the most fundamental factors in the success of any organization and one of the subjects most talked about. Yet, too often, the discussion is vague, unfocused, and ultimately unhelpful. Much of the literature on leadership starts in the middle—about what you *do* as a leader—usually with but a cursory nod to basic assumptions about what leaders actually *are* and why they are needed. Too often, leading is this big abstraction. How many times do you hear leadership discussed in simple, straightforward, *foundational* terms? Even dictionary definitions of leadership tend to be self-referential; that is, they tend to say the leader is someone who…leads. Here are some examples from various dictionaries:

Leader:

1. One who leads (*The Oxford English Dictionary*)

2. A party member chosen to manage party activities in a legislative body[12] (Merriam-Webster.com)

Leadership:

1. The dignity, office, or position of a leader…also, ability to lead (*The Oxford English Dictionary*)

2. The position or function of a leader (Dictionary.com)

3. Ability to lead (Dictionary.com)

---

12 Note the synonymous use of the terms "management" and "leader."

4. An act or instance of leading; guidance; direction (Dictionary. com)

5. The leaders of a group (Dictionary.com)

6. The office or position of a leader (Merriam-Webster.com)

7. The capacity to lead (Merriam-Webster.com)

8. The act or an instance of leading (Merriam-Webster.com)

On another web site, MindTools.com, promising "essential tools for an excellent career" I found:

- Leaders are people who do the right thing

- The word "leadership" can bring to mind......

- Leadership: a Definition--...an effective leader is a person who does the following...

These sources keep defining leadership in terms of various things people *do* or characteristics they *have*, but a real definition remains elusive.

The Armed Forces Officer is an interservice publication aimed at the new officer. The manual, defining "the common ethical core of all officers," notes that leadership has many facets and that "leadership is the art of creating a willing followership for a common cause that may appear impossible." It encourages the military officer to "reflect on the timeless themes outlined in this book and consider what honor, integrity, selflessness, commitment, and the greater good mean to you,"[13] advice relevant not just in the military but in all walks of life. A sensible start.

It turns out, then, not to be that simple to pin down just what leadership is. The Russian for leadership is *rukovodstvo*, from the roots of the words for leading by the hand. In Latin, the word is *ductus*, which means drawing, in the sense of a ductile material that is pulled and shaped. Maybe the

---

13 Department of Defense, *The Armed Forces Officer*, DOD GEN 36A, January 2006: 15.

ancient Hittites—Indo-Europeans whose empire at its height about 3,500 years ago extended across a good part of Asia Minor and the Middle East—knew how to frame things more concisely than we do today: their term for leader, *peran huwai*, literally means "the one who runs in front."[14] The afore-mentioned Christopher Kolenda quotes Lord Moran, a British Army doctor in the First World War, to the effect that leadership in the practical sense is "the capacity to frame plans which will succeed and the faculty of persuading others to carry them out in the face of death."[15] To paraphrase former Supreme Court Justice Potter Stewart's famous observation on obscenity—while we may have trouble defining leadership, we feel confident we can recognize it when we see it. Given this difficulty in precisely defining leadership, it would seem useful to take the time to lay a concrete foundation, to boil the issue down to its most basic premises. Let's step through a couple of very fundamental questions: Why do we need leaders? What is the function of a leader?

WHY DO WE NEED LEADERS?

This one seems to be pretty straightforward:

- Some task needs to be done.

- The task is challenging—not straightforward or easy

- The task requires more than one person to accomplish.

- The task requires integrated action within the organization and perhaps without.

- The effort needs to be efficiently organized.

- The task must be accomplished quickly, competently, and safely.

---

14 Sara E. Kimball, Winfred P. Lehmann, and Jonathan Slocum, *Hittite Online*, Lesson 10, http://www.utexas.edu/cola/centers/lrc/eieol/hitol-10-X.html#L123.

15 Lord Moran, *The Anatomy of Courage* (Garden City Park, NY: Avery, 1987).

Ergo: someone needs to be in charge (i.e., we need a "leader").

Think about the difference the leadership of Winston Churchill made to the free world as Europe was dragged inexorably into the Second World War. The Nazis repeatedly tested the resolve of the Continental powers, remilitarizing the Rhineland, annexing the Sudetenland, and finally invading France. British Prime Minister Neville Chamberlain and King George VI both believed the German war machine was unstoppable and that the best they could hope for was a *modus vivendi* with Germany, ceding the continent to Hitler in a desperate attempt to stave off an invasion of Britain. It was Churchill who stubbornly maintained that an assault on the freedom of any of us was an assault on the freedom of all of us, insisting in the darkest days of the summer of 1940 that Britain could—indeed must—fight. Were it not for his single-minded vision, courage, and determination—his leadership—the history of the world would be vastly different, and much of the Western world might now live in slavery under Nazi rule. In a speech before Parliament on June 4, 1940, the Prime Minister laid out his vision with classic rhetorical power:

Even though large tracts of Europe and many old and famous States have fallen or may fall into the grip of the Gestapo and all the odious apparatus of Nazi rule, we shall not flag or fail. We shall go on to the end, we shall fight in France, we shall fight on the seas and oceans,
we shall fight with growing confidence and growing strength in the air,
we shall defend our Island, whatever the cost may be,
we shall fight on the beaches,
we shall fight on the landing grounds,
we shall fight in the fields and in the streets,
we shall fight in the hills;
we shall never surrender, and even if, which I do not for a moment believe, this Island or a large part of it were

subjugated and starving, then our Empire beyond the seas, armed and guarded by the British Fleet, would carry on the struggle, until, in God's good time, the New World, with all its power and might, steps forth to the rescue and the liberation of the old.[16]

WHAT IS THE FUNCTION OF A LEADER?

Coalitions are like committees: their accomplishments tend to proceed at the pace of the least committed (or most obstructive) member.

Robert Heiler,
Executive Director
Institute for Advanced Strategic and Political Studies, Israel

The next step in this chain of reasoning is to ask what is the "function" of this necessary leader. The following is an attempt at a working definition—a pragmatic description, a point of departure.

A leader is someone who is able to

- perform the strategic analysis to conceive how to accomplish the mission assigned;

- assemble a group to accomplish a task;

- articulate the task to the team and link it to the organization's overall mission and the leader's vision;

---

16 Speech to the House of Commons of the British Parliament, June 4, 1940.

- create the conditions under which the task can be completed and under which her troops can reach their maximum potential—individually and collectively;

- ensure that the resources necessary to carry out the task are available;

- train and otherwise prepare the team for the task; and then

- "lead" or guide the team through to successful completion of that task, whatever the challenges, obstacles, and setbacks.

WHAT ARE PEOPLE LOOKING FOR IN A LEADER?

Fame is a vapor, popularity an accident, riches take wing, and only character endures.

Horace Greeley,
Nineteenth-century New York newspaper editor

Let's look briefly at how people perceive leaders and what they're looking for. As I said earlier, in almost every case, each of us is at the same time a leader and a follower; so it breaks down into two perspectives: What are your superiors looking for when they select a leader? What are "the led" looking for in a leader?

What Are Your Superiors Looking For In Their Leaders?

Or: Why in the world would they dare entrust their important project to *you*?

In the workplace, there are legions of intelligent, hardworking people whose efforts are critically important to mission success. But in the strategic sense, what always seems to be in short supply is someone who can make things happen—a closer. The one making it happen is…a leader. I've been on any number of selection panels for senior leadership over the years, and these panels are always looking for the same things, the same qualities, the same ability to get the job done. Regrettably, the list of candidates that bear these qualifications is often dishearteningly short.

Not surprisingly, it is again the Marine Corps that provides some useful perspective on what they're looking for in their young, up-and-coming leaders. The Marines talk about "the strategic corporal" in recognition of the fact that, with the battlespace becoming more dynamic and fluid, there will frequently not be enough time for small-unit leaders to radio back to Headquarters for guidance. The decisions taken in the heat of the moment by junior Non-Commissioned Officers can end up affecting—for better or worse—national policy and precipitating events that require the attention of the commanding officer, if not the President. With this in mind, the Marines, committed to inculcating leadership through the ranks, prepare their leaders to decentralize command and push decision-making down to the lowest workable level. They manage by end state, expecting their field leaders to know the plan and have the confidence to make decisions in a fluid combat environment. They want their leaders to be aggressive, confident, and analytic; able to size up the situation; determine a course of action; and execute.[17] They expect to be able to give them a mission—the "what-to"—and trust them to figure out the "how-to." Nature of mission aside, this process is no less applicable elsewhere in the government and in the private sector.

In a short but insightful book on the values he learned in the Marines, former Georgia governor Zell Miller talks about a friend who described three kinds of people: "the few who make things happen; the greater few who watch the lesser few who make things happen and then criticize; and the vast multitudes who do not know anything has happened until it is already over and done."[18] While Miller concedes that this may be a bit overstated, you—as a leader—are expected to be one of those few who are making things happen.

While not strictly dealing with recruitment of leaders per se, it's instructive to read the "help wanted" poster that Sir Ernest Shackleton is said to have used to attract a crew for his 1914 Imperial Trans-Antarctic Expedition. (The authenticity of this ad is much disputed but, as journalists say, "The story's too good to check.")

Men wanted for hazardous journey. Small wages. Bitter cold. Long months of complete darkness. Constant danger. Safe return doubtful. Honour and recognition in case of success.

Imagine that this text is running through the head of the person interviewing you for your next job. Do you have the integrity, dedication, fortitude, resourcefulness, and just plain grit to see their mission through to completion?

---

17 David H. Greedman, *Corps Business: The 30 Management Principles of the U.S. Marines* (New York: Harper Business, 2000).

18 Zell Miller, *Corps Values: Everything You Need to Know I Learned in the Marines* (Atlanta, GA: Longstreet, 1996).

What Are "The Led" Looking For In A Leader?

Or: Why in the world would they want to follow *you*?

Imagine you could line up all your old bosses:

- Which one would you most like to work for?

- What did she do to lead?

- Did you like him? Did it matter?

- Why did you want to continue to work for her—or why didn't you?

- To which leader would you most enthusiastically entrust yourself?

Now turn these questions around, and ask yourself how your team would answer these questions in regard to you. Particularly, given an arduous or dangerous mission, what would motivate people to put themselves—their professional future, their safety, perhaps even their lives—in your hands? What are they looking for in a leader? By what right, they will ask, do you sit at the head of the table? Who are you, and what have you done to warrant control of their destiny? Given a choice of leader, would they choose to follow you? It takes a great deal, would you not agree? To merit this allegiance, you must embody some set of admirable characteristics or traits. If you do, it means you will somehow have captured their confidence, and it means you are a leader. So what are these characteristics?

Basically, people are looking for someone to lead them into action, a person with whom they will succeed in their mission; someone who will get them back safe; someone who will ensure they can keep having equally or even more rewarding experiences. As a leader, you also have to be a role model so you can help your troops develop into leaders themselves—another of your major responsibilities.

Next, the overwhelming majority of people want to feel good about themselves, to feel that what they are doing has some significance. Some years ago, my wife and I owned a vehicle with four-wheel drive. With some regularity, the Washington, DC, area was hit by one of those massive snowstorms that shut the place down for a couple of days. (Actually, the snow was usually pretty light, but DC is woefully ill prepared to handle it, so life came to a halt.) We would head off to a volunteer center to be dispatched to outlying areas to bring doctors, patients, and other essential personnel into town. It was remarkable how many people showed up and how determined, how excited they were to help. These events left a lasting impression on me that there is a compelling desire in people to experience the deep gratification of doing something meaningful. It can be powerful, therefore, if your troops can identify with your vision, if you can articulate the mission—and their part in its prosecution—as something for the greater good, something they can be proud of, something bigger than themselves.

So are you a person of integrity, a person your followers can trust to put mission and their interests above your own? And can you get them across the goal line? (After all, in the end, no matter how ethical and inspiring a leader you are, if they do not see you as professionally competent enough to lead them through to mission accomplishment, they will not want to follow.)

WHAT ARE THE ELEMENTS OF LEADERSHIP?

Character is an essential tendency. It can be covered up, it can be messed with, it can be screwed around with, but it can't be ultimately changed. It's the structure of our bones, the blood that runs through our veins.

Sam Shepard,
American actor/playwright

Extrapolating from the above, then, leadership comprises three basic elements, without which it cannot be truly effective. These are

- character—integrity and purity of motive;

- vision—the ability to set a course of action against a difficult task; and

- effectiveness—the ability to successfully implement this vision and accomplish the mission.

I wrote earlier of the difficulty of defining "leader" and "leadership." Even after completing all the research for this book and writing it, I find it no easier. The terms are simply too broad and encompass so many facets of so many different dimensions of so many different aspects of life and work that I have come to the conclusion that we will never be able to pin it down to a precise set of phrases. When I see people defining leadership, I see them listing behaviors, traits, and attitudes without really capturing the whole of the concept. Here's one example where the author starts to define leadership and falls instead into describing the *behaviors* of a leader, not what leadership *is*: "Leadership can be hard to define and it means different things to different people." So the reader waits to see how the author will define it:

In the transformational leadership model, leaders set direction and help themselves and others to do the right thing to move forward. To do this they create an inspiring vision, and then motivate and inspire others to reach that vision. They also manage delivery of the vision, either directly or indirectly, and build and coach their teams to make them ever stronger.[19]

---

19 "What Is Leadership," Mind Tools, http://www.mindtools.com/pages/article/newLDR_41.htm. (accessed 13 April 2015.)

Again, these are all legitimate traits and behaviors, but a definition, per se, continues to elude us. My effort here will probably be no better, so rather than devoting too much time to trying to define what's in the box, I'm going to put the frame around the box and spend the rest of the book trying to fill in enough narrative and examples that you can come up with your own definition...or perhaps an ability to apply intuition and a set of behaviors and responses you can draw on in leadership situations, vice pulling out the laminated card with the simple three-line definition on it. In the meantime, here's a working definition that I use:

Leadership: *the panoply[20] of values, skills, traits, and behaviors that enable one to induce and inspire others to act effectively according to one's intent in furtherance of mission accomplishment.*

With this definition proposed, now let's explore character and leadership in greater detail.

---

20 I've used the word *panoply* here intentionally. The word comes from the ancient Greek, meaning literally "all arms." It was the full kit of helmet, breastplate, shield, spear, and other gear that the Greek hoplite infantryman carried into battle. I like the sense that the leader is armed with values, skills, traits, and behaviors—all those things that equip him to accomplish his mission.

Chapter 2

CHARACTER IN LEADERSHIP

The qualities of a great man are vision, integrity, courage, understanding, the power of articulation, and profundity of character.

President Dwight D. Eisenhower

WHAT CONSTITUTES THE CHARACTER OF A LEADER?

To start off, give some thought to this question: Why do you want to be a leader? Is it for prestige? Glory? Money? Your own advancement? In the Intelligence Community and the larger defense establishment, I think the answer really has to be patriotism and a desire to serve and protect the nation. So what is your motivation? Why would you be there wanting to be a leader? Public recognition? A paycheck? If you're reading this book, I suspect that's not your motivation.

Recently, a friend showed me a book by Robert Greene entitled *The 48 Laws of Power*. According to Wikipedia (for reasons that will become clear shortly, I didn't buy the book), Greene uses anecdotes from historical figures of the iron-fist school, such as Louis XIV, Bismarck, Mao Zedong, and Machiavelli, to illustrate real-world application of his forty-eight rules. This kind of scorched-earth leadership book is all the rage these days, like *Downward Feedback Rolls Downhill: The Human Resources Secrets of Attila the Hun*. They seem clever, and they suggest that you can cut throats, stab backs, and claw and lie your way to the top. Green's "laws" are so ludicrous that at first I thought the list was a parody. If you could get further afield than 180 degrees from the right approach, this book would be that—squared. Just take a look at some of the rules:

- Never outshine the master.

- Never put too much trust in friends; learn how to use enemies.

- Conceal your intentions.

- Court attention at all cost.

- Get others to do the work for you, but always take the credit.

- Learn to keep people dependent on you.

- Use selective honesty and generosity to disarm your victim.

- Pose as a friend; work as a spy.

- Crush your enemy totally.

- Keep others in suspended terror; cultivate an air of unpredictability.

- Do not commit to anyone.

- Play to people's fantasies.

- Discover each man's thumbscrew.

- Be royal in your own fashion: act like a king to be treated like one.

- Avoid stepping into a great man's shoes.

These strike me as the life rules of a sociopath. Maybe if you're a *realpolitik*ing Metternich or Bismarck, playing on the world stage, these tactics could be useful, but not for those of us playing triple-A ball. Someone in my organization operating according to these rules wouldn't last two minutes. I can't imagine anyone wanting to work for, with, or over someone who behaved like this. While we can all point to people in senior positions (I won't dignify them by calling them leaders) who are such skilled sociopaths that they can seduce, cheat, and lie their way to the top, no one that I count as a friend could go home and look himself in the mirror if he conducted himself according to these "laws." I would hope most of us would rather be a penniless, jobless failure than resort to the tactics that Greene advocates. If you want a quick leadership checklist, download Greene's list of forty-eight laws, put a "not" in front of them, print them on a laminated card, and act accordingly. You'll be a paragon of virtue, probably more successful in your work, and at the very least, you'll be able to face your mother without embarrassment.

Some years ago, I came across a far better book, a book that has become one of my favorites. I think I've probably given away more than a hundred copies over the years to friends and colleagues in my Program. It is *Gates of Fire*, a historical novel about ancient Greece, written by Steven Pressfield (notably a former Marine). It deals with the Battle of Thermopylae in 480 BC, in which a force of three hundred Spartans, backed by warriors from allied city-states, held off the hoards of the Persian king, Xerxes, for three days—a lesson of courage, sacrifice, and duty that has remained an inspiration for two and a half millennia. Curious how this small band of Spartans held fast for three days in the face of determined assault by his elite troops, Xerxes has the lone Spartan survivor brought to his tent so he can question him. The narrative device of the book is a retrospective by this survivor (who was actually not a warrior but something of a training assistant) on the nature of Spartan society and particularly the *agoge*, the arduous thirteen-year program that molded Spartan boys into the most powerful military force of their time. Shortly before he succumbs to his wounds, the survivor struggles to prop himself up on an elbow to, ironically, explain to the King what a king is. This passage is simply *the best, the most concise description of leadership* I have ever encountered. If you do nothing else to develop yourself as a leader, simply substitute *leader* for *king* here and resolve to live your life according to these lines:

Of what does the nature of kingship consist? What are its qualities in itself; what are the qualities it inspires in those who attend it? These, if one may presume to divine the meditations of His Majesty's heart, are the questions which most preoccupy his own reason and reflection.

I will tell His Majesty what a king is.

A king does not abide within his tent while his men bleed and die upon the field.

A king does not dine while his men go hungry, nor sleep when they stand at watch upon the wall.

A king does not command his men's loyalty through fear nor purchase it with gold; he earns their love by the sweat of his own back and the pains he endures for their sake.

That which comprises the harshest burden, a king lifts first and sets down last.

A king does not require service of those he leads but provides it to them. He serves them, not they him.

That, Your Majesty, is a king.[21]

I think this passage is so remarkable that I want to go over it line by line and ask you to relate it to our times and your particular organization.

A king does not abide within his tent while his men bleed and die upon the field.

A leader leads from the front. Those being led want to see that the leader is willing to take the same risks that he or she is asking of them (if not more). These risks need not be confined to physical danger. They can include operational threats, or even bureaucratic head-butting. While you need to be leading and, therefore, can't always be on the ground grinding it out with your team, you need to spend some time with them to show you're willing to bleed and suffer alongside them. You need to *radiate* respect for them and what they do (more on this later). You need to carefully follow what they're up to, the challenges they're facing, rather than spending all your time on your computer answering e-mails or briefing up the chain. Believe me, your "hall file"—your uncensored watercooler reputation—will follow you, and people will know your true nature. If you haven't put your time in at the front (physically or bureaucratically), slugging it out alongside your troops, that reputation will follow you. If you have always led from the front, that too will be remembered. Whatever senior management thinks—whoever gets promoted, whoever gets the face time with the front office—the troops will always know the good guys from the bad. If you're perceived as cowering in the back, they will unfailingly know it; you will lose all respect, and...you are *not* a leader.

---

21 Steven Pressfield, *Gates of Fire* (New York: Doubleday, 1988): 360.

A king does not dine while his men go hungry, nor sleep when they stand at watch upon the wall.

More of the same. If you are seen to be hogging the perks for yourself and not caring about—and caring for—your team, you are *not* a leader, and they will *not* follow. There are many stories from the military about how officers or Non-Coms will go short on food or equipment in the interest of ensuring their troops get what they need. If you're (figuratively) eating better chow, or sleeping in a drier tent, or feeling you deserve better because of your higher position…you are *not* a leader.

Earlier I mentioned one of history's greatest examples of courage and endurance under extreme conditions: the 1914–1916 British Imperial Trans-Antarctic Expedition, led by Sir Ernest Shackleton. When the expedition's ship, *Endurance*, became trapped in the ice and was later crushed, the crew of twenty-eight managed to survive for two years until they finally made it back to civilization. Shackleton's leadership during this grueling ordeal is one of the classic examples of the need for, and power of, true leadership. A telling example was the distribution of sleeping bags when the crew was finally forced to abandon the ship and establish a camp on the ice. There were only eighteen of the warmer animal-skin sleeping bags, the rest being wool. The crew drew lots for the bags. As recorded by one of the crew: "There was some crooked work in the drawing." Shackleton and the other officers all drew wool bags, while the warmer fur bags all went to the men under them.[22] Despite two grueling years on the ice, Shackleton brought home every member of his crew alive.

A king does not command his men's loyalty through fear nor purchase it with gold; he earns their love by the sweat of his own back and the pains he endures for their sake.

---

22 WGBH, "Shackleton's Leadership Role," http://main.wgbh.org/imax/shackleton/shackleton. html. (accessed September 2013).

You can be *appointed to* a position of leadership, but *no one above can bestow the title "leader" upon you; it can only be earned from those being led.* Managers can be appointed; leaders cannot. While you may have the authority on paper to demand that they turn to, the approach of "don't ask why; just do it because I say so" will fail in the end (if not sooner). You cannot lead through intimidation or fear, or by simply pointing to the rank insignia on your collar. That's not leadership, and they'll abandon you at the first opportunity. To paraphrase the Declaration of Independence, *leadership must ultimately derive its just power from the consent of those being led.*

That which comprises the harshest burden, a king lifts first and sets down last.

I recall vividly when I was promoted to the senior executive service (essentially the equivalent of military flag officer) and failed to evade the dreaded "charm course" for budding new executives. We went out of town for one of those excruciating "off-sites," a revolting weeklong orgy of self-congratulation about how "special" we were. Instead, they should have sat us down with a copy of *Gates of Fire* and drilled into us: "Welcome to the senior service. You had it good before, when you could defer responsibility to others. Now, the onus is on you. This should be a very sobering occasion. There are no skirts to hide behind now. You have ascended to a position of significant responsibility and accountability (never mind authority or power). Your team, the organization, and the American people expect you to work harder, think bolder, act more courageously—to make things happen. Forget about the executive dining room, more pay, and a better parking space. Forget about the "prestige" of the senior service. Forget about executive-floor face time. You will be expected to inspire your people, keep them safe, and deliver the goods. Now get back to work." In forty-seven years with the organization, I have regrettably never heard my responsibilities defined quite this directly, this bluntly. You hear it now from me.

A king does not require service of those he leads but provides it to them. He serves them, not they him.

This is an extremely important point that is often missed, if not downright contradicted by many so-called leaders. Think about it: as you progress to a leadership level, you will be less and less involved in the hands-on accomplishment of the mission. Your job as a leader, then, is to *create the conditions* that allow those doing the real work to succeed—to *serve* them. When briefing on the Program that I manage, I frequently draw the organization chart upside down from the way you would usually imagine it—the field teams on top, supported by the inverted pyramid of analytic and technical support elements, Headquarters line elements, staffs, and other senior leaders, with me—the Program Manager—at the bottom. The message is that we're all essentially a support infrastructure whose sole function is to prepare, dispatch, and then sustain our team in the field. Whatever it takes to that end, we will do.

These principles of leadership were well understood by great leaders millennia ago. One can go at least as far back as Alexander the Great (356–323 BC) for recognition of the qualities described above. Alexander was famous for being at the head of the charge or the first into the breech, inspiring courage and fierce devotion in his men. The Greek historian Arian[23] extolled these virtues in *The Campaigns of Alexander*, including the following:

I must not leave unrecorded one of the finest things Alexander ever did...The army was crossing a desert of sand; the sun was already blazing down upon them, but they were struggling on under the necessity of reaching water, which was still far away. Alexander,

23 Arrian, or Lucius Flavius Arrianus (AD ca. 86–ca. 160), was a Greek, born of aristocratic parents, who became a Roman citizen and ultimately reached the rank of consul and, later, governor of the province of Capadocia. He studied philosophy under the Stoic Epictetus and famously cataloged his teaching in *Discourses*. He also wrote a number of military and historical treatises, the most famous of which is his history of Alexander's campaigns.

like everyone else, was tormented by thirst, but he was none the less marching on foot at the head of his men. It was all he could do to keep going, but he did so, and the result (as always) was that the men were better able to endure their misery when they saw that it was equally shared.... A party of light infantry which had gone off looking for water found some—just a wretched little trickle collected in a shallow gully. They scooped up with difficulty what they could and hurried back, with their priceless treasure to Alexander; then, just before they reached him, they tipped the water into a helmet and gave it to him. Alexander, with a word of thanks for the gift, took the helmet and, in full view of his troops, poured the water on the ground. So extraordinary was the effect of this action that the water wasted by Alexander was as good as a drink for every man in the army. I cannot praise this act too highly; it was proof, in anything was, not only of his power of endurance, but also of his genius for leadership. [24]

Whatever his faults, and they were many, Alexander is unarguably one of the great military leaders of history. He led from the front, shared his men's hardships, and inspired them through word and deed. It is significant that Arian, a senior military and political leader in the early Roman Empire, recognized and esteemed these same leadership behaviors that we still value today.

---

24 Arrian, *The Campaigns of Alexander* (New York: Penguin Classics, 1971): 338-339

Chapter 3

THE TRAITS OF A LEADER

Character cannot be developed in ease and quiet. Only through experience of trial and suffering can the soul be strengthened, vision cleared, ambition inspired, and success achieved.

Helen Keller

While there exist an infinity of definitions, checklists, and "secrets" of leadership out there, in the end, no one can hand it to you on a platter. Like all those things of value in life, leadership is something you have to work at, constantly refining your understanding of yourself, your mission, your team. But people like checklists so, for better or worse, here are *but a few* of the qualities that characterize a true leader. Shared values like these help focus your organization's efforts toward a common objective, give it cohesion, and ultimately enable you to achieve mission success. But remember, it's not enough just to *be* these things. Part of being a leader is demonstration. You must *be seen* to have these qualities; you must consciously ensure that the troops understand who you are and what you stand for. Every day, you must earn their respect and loyalty if they are to follow you. Make no mistake—they will be watching you and taking your measure. You may not be naturally outgoing but, like it or not, you're always onstage, and you must find ways to ensure your troops understand what kind of person you are and what your values are, and that they can see in you someone they can safely entrust themselves to. It's tremendously effective when they see their leader climb down into the trenches and spend time with the troops, praising great performance and getting underperformers back on track. On the other hand, if your troops never see you, if you delegate those interactions to others, if you cloister yourself and direct your attention upward toward the executive suite, your effectiveness as a leader will be fatally compromised.

Your troops must be in no doubt about your character, your values, your work ethic, your professionalism, your priorities, your skills. And I'm not talking about acting; this demonstration must be the real thing. (I'm making an important distinction here: some people are naturally outgoing; others are more introverted. It's not that you can't be a leader unless you are the proverbial hail-fellow-well-met. If you happen to be an introvert, it just means you have to work hard at these social interactions; *acting* in this sense does not imply that it's not sincere, just that it doesn't come particularly naturally. Plenty of great leaders have been introverts. Just don't use it as an excuse to avoid these vital interactions with the troops.)

So here are some of the traits of a leader, not necessarily in order of importance. You will note that many of these traits are overlapping and interrelated. I'll list them first then address each in more detail. And relax, no one is going to excel in all of these traits, but they do all merit constant attention, contemplation, and effort.

Integrity

Courage

Selflessness

Competence

Rhetoric

Grace

Justice

Respect

Vision

Tolerance for honest mistakes

Work ethic/persistence

Passion

Initiative

Reliability

Maturity

Judgment

Decisiveness

INTEGRITY

Forge thy tongue on an anvil of truth and what flies up, though it be a spark, shall have weight.

Pindar,
Greek lyric poet, ca. 522–443 BC

Think about what this timeless quote means. If you don't have integrity, that means you are not trustworthy—literally, *not worthy of others' trust.* If they can't trust you, don't expect them to follow you into action; forget being a leader. On the other hand, if you have developed a reputation for honesty and integrity, when the chips are down, you will have the credibility you need to lead the way.

The question is often asked: Can you separate private from professional morality? Many people disagree, but I don't think you can. Theodore Roosevelt is reputed to have said, "To educate a person in mind and not in morals is to educate a menace to society." If people see a leader as lacking in honor, being self-promoting, or lying to get ahead in his private life, why should they expect him to reorder his priorities in a professional setting? If she strays from the path, why shouldn't they, too? The troops are quick to pick up on the hypocrite who talks a good game but doesn't live up to what she's preaching. So people will look at you with this question in mind and make their assessment. Without a reputation for integrity, you're on thin ice. On the other hand, if you establish that trust, you can do anything, and they will do anything for you.

Another important point: trust in leadership is not automatic; it takes a long time to build up but is astonishingly easy to squander. Think of integrity as similar to physical fitness: if you don't work every day to maintain it, it can quickly atrophy. Your troops must understand that you set high standards for your personal conduct and expect them to do the same *every day*.

As usual, Shakespeare said it best, this time in *Hamlet*. Polonius, the Lord Chamberlain of the king's court, is giving some last-minute advice to his son, Laertes, before he heads off to school. This entire passage is timeless wisdom, but the words on integrity are truly unforgettable:

This above all: to thine own self be true,
and it must follow, as the night the day,
Thou canst not then be false to any man.

The signers of the Declaration of Independence pledged their lives, their fortunes, and their sacred honor in the fight to win independence, the same independence and freedom for which we are fighting today. Live a life of honor and integrity; don't put your personal interests before the mission and your people; know the difference between right and wrong and act accordingly; be good for your word. Your integrity is your honor. Guard it with your life for, without integrity and honor, no matter what your grade, position, or salary, the fulfillment you are looking for will not come, and...you are *not* a leader.

COURAGE

If you have men who will only come if they know there is a good road, I don't want them. I want men who will come if there is no road at all.

David Livingstone,
Scottish missionary and explorer, 1813–1874

Courage is a term most often thought about in the physical sense...as overcoming fear in the face of danger. Thankfully most readers will not be practicing their leadership in life-threatening circumstances, but that doesn't mean that there will not be situations in which you will need to summon up the courage to face a big challenge. I'm talking not only about a degree of physical courage but, equally important, about mental or moral courage, the courage of your convictions, standing up for what is right even if it is not popular, even if you have to face off against authority. After all, if *you* don't believe in what you're doing, why should your team? If *you* don't feel strongly enough about risking yourself for this mission, why should they? If *you* try to push them out in front to face the risk alone, why would you think they would want to have anything to do with you?

I'd also like to offer a critical point about what I see as one of the principal reasons we sometimes struggle to come up with the best performance (and, regrettably, this affliction is not limited to the Intelligence Community). You can arguably fault a lot of things: resources, loss of experienced officers, and so forth, but a major factor today is that we suffer from its being too easy to say no in the face of the seemingly impossible. And you aren't going to tackle today's hard missions without venturing into territory that most believe is impossible. I have seen situations in the past where "the establishment" has refused approval for an

29

operation, saying, "No way, that's impossible; we would get caught; it's too hard." And there is no penalty for this. The ones who must put their heads in the noose are the ones willing to step up to the risk. They run all the bureaucratic risk, with little potential for personal gain, while the naysayers rarely suffer for their timidity. What kind of behavior does that incentivize? The leader—be she in government, business, medicine, academia, education, or military service—must teach her people to size up the risk; deal with fear; and summon the physical, mental, and moral courage to forge ahead rather than shy away.

I'll give you another example—of bad leadership in this case—from the highest levels of the Intelligence Community. Some years ago, we brought on-line a first-of-a-kind operation of great importance, at great cost, and at considerable risk to our personnel. The whole undertaking had been fraught with controversy and dissention, some of it pretty ugly. Late in the game, a new supervisor came in determined to close it down. After about a year of bloody bureaucratic fighting, the call was referred to the man at the top—a man, in my opinion, with an ego inversely proportional to his moral backbone. The final decision was supposed to come at a meeting of seniors from the top of several intelligence organizations, held at the White House. I started out with a briefing on the background and status of the operation, and then the chief polled those around the table. Opinions were mixed. With everyone sitting on the edge of his chair waiting for the decision, the chief dropped his size-fifteen shoes from the table (where he had stuck them with typical arrogance in everyone's face), leaned forward, and gave his decision. You could have cut the tension with the proverbial knife. What did he say? "I think I'm going to hand this over to my deputy to decide." The deputy, a great and widely respected leader, looked as if he'd been kicked in the stomach. Everyone was astonished and angry. All I could think about was the Chosin Reservoir. In June 1950, communist North Korea invaded the South, quickly overrunning South Korean defenses. After initially being pushed into a small pocket in the very south of the Korean peninsula, South Korean and United Nations forces counterattacked and pushed north, eventually reaching an area close to the Chinese border. At that point, Communist China entered the war, launching a massive attack across the Yalu River, sending the UN forces reeling. These units, including the 1st Marine Division, were surrounded by more than sixty thousand Chinese troops near the infamous "Frozen Chosin," in brutal, subzero temperatures. Over seventeen days in November and December 1950, the UN forces broke the encirclement and withdrew south. The Marines, particularly, withdrew in good order, with their casualties and equipment, inflicting crippling losses on the Chinese. The battle went into Marine Corps history, in the process spawning another of those marvelous quotes from Marine Corps legend Chesty Puller, perhaps apocryphal, but characteristic of what he would say nonetheless: "We've been looking for the enemy for some time now. We've finally found him. We're surrounded. That simplifies things. We can fire in all directions."[25]

I had this in mind when our chief threw the hot potato over to his deputy. I could just imagine the Marine commanding general—standing in the freezing snow, receiving reports about the latest Chinese attack—with all his staff surrounding him, saying, "I think I'll hand this decision over to my deputy." He would have been relieved by the next morning. What little regard we had for the chief up to that point dissolved on the spot. The deputy went on to make the hard call and, to this day, he commands the greatest respect from all who served with him.

Leaders, in whatever field, must create a culture in which daring "operations" are given due consideration—subject, of course, to rigorous analysis and hard-nosed risk/gain trades. Team leaders need to conceive and recommend such courses of action, and senior leaders need to back them, *particularly when things go awry*. (It's easy to support the troops in the face of victory.)

---

25 Martin Russ, *Breakout: The Chosin Reservoir Campaign, Korea, 1950* (New York: Penguin, 2000).

Famously, General Dwight Eisenhower drafted a statement for issuance in the event that the D-Day invasion of Normandy, the largest amphibious operation in history, failed. Eisenhower, a true leader, understood that this monumental undertaking, and the fate of more than 160,000 US and Allied combatants rested squarely on his shoulders. The statement leaves no doubt that Eisenhower was prepared to assume full responsibility in case of disaster. His note, shown below, represents the epitome of leadership. Less courageous commanders, in the wake of failed operations, have looked for every excuse to point the finger of blame in the direction of others. Not Eisenhower. He had the courage to accept responsibility. Contrast him to the chief I described above.

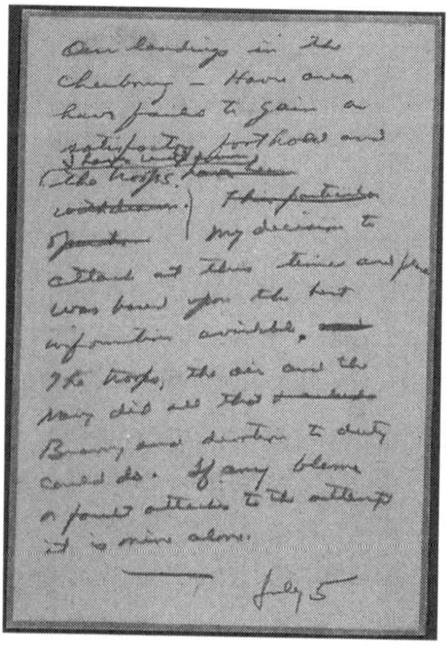

Our landings in the Cherburg-Havre area have failed to gain a satisfactory foothold and I have withdrawn the troops. My decision to attack at this time and place was based on the best information available. The troops, the air and the navy did all that Bravery and devotion to duty could do. If any blame or fault attaches to the attempt it is mine alone.

July 5

Figure 1. The statement that Eisenhower drafted for release in case of failure on D-Day.[26]

---

26 In Case of Failure Message, Butcher Diary June 28–July 14, 1944, Principal File, Box 168, pp. 2, Eisenhower's Pre-Presidential Papers, Eisenhower Presidential Library, Museum and Boyhood Home, Abilene, Kansas.

Again, while we perhaps first think of courage in the context of the battlefield, don't think of only the physical; there are ample occasions in normal, everyday life that demand the virtue of moral courage and leadership by example. Think of Rosa Parks, an African American seamstress living in Montgomery, Alabama, in the mid-1950s. In the early 1900s, many states in the south had enacted so-called Jim Crow laws that imposed segregation in public facilities, including buses. Hard as it may be to believe almost sixty years later, public buses were sectioned off, with seats reserved for whites only in the front, while blacks were relegated to the rear. If the whites-only section filled up, blacks were expected to vacate their seats and stand to accommodate a white person. On the first of December in 1955, the forty-two-year-old Parks refused a driver's demand that she yield her seat—in the days of racial violence and the Ku Klux Klan, no trivial feat of defiance. While she may not have been the first to so refuse, hers was an act that was to reverberate through history. Parks was arrested, jailed, and eventually found guilty of disorderly conduct. But her steadfastness served as the catalyst for a boycott of public buses, organized by Montgomery's black churches. The boycott lasted 381 days and led to the repeal of the laws that mandated segregation of public transportation. While Parks probably never considered herself a leader or had the specific intention to serve as a role model, her personal courage inspired not only African Americans, but also a growing number of white Americans to oppose segregation writ large. For her courage and leadership, in the bus boycott and in subsequent service to the civil rights movement, Parks received a number of local and national awards, including the National Association for the Advancement of Colored People's Spingarn Medal, the Congressional Gold Medal, and the Presidential Medal of Freedom, the highest civilian honor for service to the country. Perhaps one of the most telling comments about her leadership was spoken by then–Secretary of State Condoleezza Rice who said that, without the inspiration of Parks' courage, she might never have become Secretary of State. Unarguably, courage comes in all forms, sizes, races, and genders.

In sum, a good leader (even if not at the moment in a *position* of leadership) must have the courage of her convictions. Stand up for what you believe in; don't be reticent to voice your opinion, even if you think it might be unpopular. You can be a leader even if you're not the designated top dog. *If* you've thought it through and *if* you think you have a case, then stand up and make it; don't hold back. For the situation at hand and for your development as a future leader, you need to develop the confidence and courage to speak up. Good leaders don't inwardly shake their heads and go back to the office, not having spoken up, and rail under their breath about how dumb management is. Good leaders work out their position and have the courage to articulate it and let the chips fall where they may.

SELFLESSNESS

When you pull on that jersey, the name on the front is a hell of a lot more important than the one on the back.

Herb Brooks,
coach of the "Miracle on Ice,"
1980 gold medal US Olympic hockey team

Selflessness is another characteristic I believe critical to effective leadership. You've heard it before in different forms: "ship, shipmate, self" ..."mission, men, me." They all say the same thing; your loyalty, your dedication, your energies are dedicated first and foremost to your mission and your team, not to your own ends. In the intelligence business, the missions and responsibilities we undertake on behalf of the American people are simply more important than we are. In your world, you won't be a true leader if you put your own interests at the head of the list. As with the other qualities we've been discussing, if your troops see you putting yourself at the center of everything, making your decisions based on personal interest, or hogging the limelight, you're toast as a leader.

Peter Senge, director of the Center for Organizational Learning at the MIT Sloan School of Management, has this to say on the subject:

> *The reliability of a combat officer's orders being followed relates directly to only one thing: the trust [soldiers] have that the leader actually cares about them as people. If they're going to put their lives at risk, they need to know they're under the command of somebody who actually does care about their lives.*[27]

Earlier, I used the term "hall file" to describe a leader's informal reputation based on watercooler talk in the hallway. Phone calls to the ratline can also be used to ferret out a more candid performance appraisal. You don't want the report on you to be something like: "He's out for himself... You can't trust him." Where I come from, careerism is one of the worst things you can accuse a colleague of. I'll concede again that there are those who are in it principally to climb the ladder, and some even eventually get to the top, but they are revealed quickly for what they are and command a commensurate minimal degree of respect from their troops. And the bottom line is if your troops don't respect you, in the end, you can't accomplish much. I've seen that proven for the most junior leaders up through the Director.

Another of my favorite reflections on character is "A Father's Prayer," which General Douglas MacArthur wrote for his young son. Controversial and idiosyncratic though the general may have been, this

---

27 Peter Senge, *The Fifth Discipline: The Art and Practice of the Learning Organization* (New York: Currency, 1990).

piece is a superb example of masterful, economical verse that delivers in six compact paragraphs (two follow below) more wisdom on character than most books do in hundreds of pages:

Build me a son whose heart will be clean, whose goal will be high; a son who will master himself before he seeks to master other men; one who will learn to laugh, yet never forget how to weep; one who will reach into the future, yet never forget the past.

And after all these things are his, add, I pray, enough of a sense of humor, so that he may always be serious, yet never take himself too seriously. Give him humility, so that he may always remember the simplicity of greatness, the open mind of true wisdom, the meekness of true strength.

Read this along with MacArthur's magnificent farewell address at West Point, "Duty, Honor, Country," delivered under a sweltering June sun when he was eighty-two, from just a few notes, hastily jotted down. Together, these two pieces represent an invaluable guide for how to live the selfless life: a life devoted to duty, honor, and country—a life of wisdom, justice, courage, and moderation.

COMPETENCE

If you have a vision without the resources to implement it, all you really have is a hallucination.

Overheard in the halls of the Pentagon

Charismatic, noble, and conscientious though you may be, if you don't know your business, no one will want to follow you to "the field." At the end of the day, you need to be effective; that's what matters, and that's what you're being hired to do. In this sense, anyway, there's no inherent value in being a person of character; you can be a great guy but, if you can't deliver, you're not really worth hiring. Colonel Thomas Kolditz, professor and head of the Department of Behavioral Sciences and Leadership at the US Military Academy at West Point, is far more eloquent on this subject than I am. In his book *In Extremis Leadership*, Kolditz writes: "When things get physically dangerous or operationally hairy, the troops want someone who *first will keep them alive* and then lead them through to success."[28] You should strive to be as good (or better) at your core competency as they are at theirs. Your record should prove that you were mission effective on your way up. You must continue to develop yourself professionally and demonstrate to your troops that you are motivated to *constantly* learn and improve your abilities, the better to lead them.

In the work of defending our nation, second place is not good enough. In the Intelligence Community, at the end of the day, we are not being paid to be leaders. We're being paid to produce results—information vital to our security and the protection of our way of life. In your world, your substantive abilities must inspire confidence. Leadership is essential to this end, but if you can't deliver the goods, leadership doesn't count for much.

RHETORIC

In Greece and Rome, eloquence was power...The voice of oratory was the thunder of Jupiter.

John Quincy Adams
Lectures on Rhetoric and Oratory, 1810

---

28 Thomas A. Kolditz, *In Extremis Leadership: Leading as If Your Life Depended on It* (San Francisco: Jossey-Bass, 2007).

Rhetoric is not usually a skill talked about in the context of leadership, but it is one of *the* most essential skills you must develop to succeed. Today, the term *rhetoric* seems to enjoy a questionable reputation in some quarters. Many now take it in a pejorative sense, to mean deceitful or manipulative speech—sophistry. In its true sense, however, it merely means the use of speech and writing to influence others. (It also does a far better job of expressing the skill than that management buzzword of the day, *communication*.) And don't confuse rhetoric with fancy speech. Rhetoric involves making your speaking and writing more effective, more persuasive, more precise, and more economical—not fancier.

Assuming that you have your vision and a plan to implement it—those first two elements of leadership—and once you recruit your team, can you clearly and precisely communicate your intent to them? After all, there are an infinite number of possible courses of action out there, and you need to be able to give your team explicit guidance about which one to follow. Can you convey a plan in a way that is precise and comprehensive enough that they will know how to act when the inevitable curveballs start coming across? Can you tie your plan to the organization's mission and motivate your team to give their all?

And can you convince senior management to back your ideas? They encounter an endless stream of managers promoting initiatives of various sorts. Why would they go for yours? Can you "make the sale"? Can you tie your vision to their strategic plan and explain how it will advance the organization's objectives? Absent that ability, your scheme will never get a chance, so...you are *not* a leader.

In sum, you must be able to clearly articulate your thoughts, intentions, and goals to your team and clearly report all these, along with your progress, problems, and so on, to your supervisors. The tool that enables you to do this is rhetoric and, like any other skill, it can be honed and polished through hard work and practice. Rhetoric gives you the ability to forge a consensus, to motivate and build confidence in your team.

Winston Churchill, one of the great rhetoricians of all time, polished his skills while serving in colonial India, where he read voraciously, often memorizing long passages from Edward Gibbon's *The Decline and Fall of the Roman Empire*. Contrary to common assumptions, he was not a born speaker; he only attained that excellence through hard work (he reportedly put eight to ten hours into preparing every speech) and a conscious determination to build this critical skill.

Read—or, even better, listen to—the speeches of Abba Eban, an Israeli who served as his country's permanent representative to the United Nations and later as Foreign Minister. In July 1956, he addressed an emergency session of the UN General Assembly in the wake of Egypt's seizure of the Suez Canal. (Israel counterattacked, and its forces would have captured the canal had the United States not obliged Israel to halt its offensive.) With powerful rhetoric, Eban meticulously laid out Israel's case, winning enthusiastic applause from an audience not known for its pro-Israeli sympathies (even so, the UN subsequently voted to force an Israeli pullback, turning a deaf ear to Eban's beautifully reasoned logic). Eban, who was reputed to be fluent in ten languages, ranks with Winston Churchill as one of the most compelling and effective orators of the twentieth century. His speeches are masterpieces of logic, organization, and persuasion—rhetoric at its best.[29]

GRACE

A high station in life is earned by the gallantry with which appalling experiences are survived with grace.

Tennessee Williams

---

29 Several of Eban's most notable speeches are available on the website of the Jewish Heritage Video Collection, http://www.jhvc.org/eban/.

Another character trait that I suspect you may never have heard used with respect to leadership is grace—proper demeanor or, simply, conducting yourself with dignity, empathy, and humility. The ability to conduct oneself with grace can be an amazingly powerful tool in the hands of a great leader. And never forget who got you there. President Dwight D. Eisenhower, a military and political leader of great integrity and accomplishment, said, "Humility must always be the portion of any man who receives acclaim earned in the blood of his followers and the sacrifices of his friends."[30]

What is grace? It covers a multitude of behaviors, but really it comes down to being considerate of others; being properly humble and grateful for your blessings; putting the interests of the mission and your people before your own; maintaining self-control under stress; and projecting an image of integrity, competence, selflessness, and humility. This may all sound corny, but we have had some very quiet, unassuming people working in our Program over the years who were paragons of grace, and they were absolutely loved by the troops and, consequently, were immensely effective—the troops would do anything for them.

It is tremendously gratifying to work with someone who lives his or her life with grace. Think about your demeanor. Ours is a world of adversity and constant change. How do you deal with hard times and the sudden reversal of fortune? When things go to hell in a handbasket, how do you deal with it? Do you accept responsibility? Or do you blame others? How do you treat others when you are under great stress? The ability to maintain a calm demeanor in the face of adversity is essential in a leader. Ernest Hemingway described guts as grace under pressure. No one wants to be led by a screamer who dissolves at the first sign of trouble or by someone who passes misery downhill to the troops. And, as always, it must be genuine; as actress Helen Nielsen said, "Humility is like underwear; essential, but indecent if it shows."

---

30 Gen. Dwight d. Eisenhower, address delivered at Guildhall, London, June 12, 1945.

JUSTICE

The best index to a person's character is (a) how he treats people who can't do him any good, and (b) how he treats people who can't fight back.

Abigail van Buren ("Dear Abby"),
advice columnist

Life is unfair, and we can't always count on getting a square deal. People today face extraordinarily challenging situations, often at some personal risk. What the troops want, what they have every right to ask for, is justice—a sense that things will be handled objectively, against some established and consistent set of rules, leavened with human understanding by leaders who have personally experienced the vagaries of life and who have used that experience to gain some broader perspective. In leadership, to paraphrase the Golden Rule, lead others as you yourself would be led. On the contrary, if over and above the normal stresses of the mission your team have to deal with uncertainties about how they will be judged and how the rules will be applied, or if you cannot convince them that the cause in which they are working is a just one, you can expect added levels of stress, distraction, and unwillingness to give their all. Again, bad leadership leads to bad performance, leads to mission failure.

RESPECT

The discipline which makes the soldiers of a free country reliable in battle is not to be gained by harsh or tyrannical treatment. On the contrary, such treatment is far more likely to destroy than to make an army. It is possible to impart instruction and give commands in such a manner and such a tone of voice as to inspire in the soldier no feeling but an intense desire to obey, while the opposite manner and tone of voice cannot fail to excite strong resentment and a desire to disobey. The one mode or the other of dealing with subordinates springs from a corresponding spirit in the breast of the commander. He who feels the respect which is due to others cannot fail to inspire in them a respect for himself. While he who feels, and hence manifests, disrespect towards others, especially his subordinates, cannot fail to inspire hatred against himself.

Major General John M. Schofield,
Address to West Point graduating class of 1879

This is a critical element, one at the source of much of the organizational and personal fractiousness you will deal with as a leader. Understand right now the overwhelming importance of respect. Everyone wants to feel respected. In my experience, almost every interagency, inter-directorate, and inter-team squabble eventually boils down to someone's feeling that he's not being shown due respect. And, as much as people want to be respected, they really, *really* don't want to feel disrespected—*dis'ed* in the current parlance. As I noted earlier, most people are looking for meaning in their lives, a feeling that they're doing something important. Mutual puzzlement at the actions of the "other" organizations notwithstanding, the vast majority see themselves as loyal Americans—intelligent, highly motivated, dedicated, and proud of what they're doing. They want to be able to respect themselves, and—whatever their role in the struggle—they want to feel that their leaders, teammates, and colleagues value them and their efforts. Work to put yourself in their position and imagine things from their point of view. As we say in our Program, "assume noble intent". You'll be right at least some of the time.

Not only does your respect for your people need to be sincere, you must constantly *demonstrate* this respect, for them and for their professionalism. It will be important that you have a firsthand feel for what they do. Go into "the field" with them, and take a crack at it yourself. Show a genuine interest in what your troops do. Get down in the dirt with them. You cannot be expected to be an expert in every skill set under your command, but you need to show that you have a good understanding of the critical part each person plays in mission success and that you appreciate how much hard work and dedication it took them to reach their skill level. Even though you may not match their level of competence in their specialty, they'll welcome your interest and will be anxious to demonstrate their competence (truth be told, they rather enjoy being better at it than you are).

Practice with your team; let them see your interest in understanding the complexities and the nuances of their tasks. Having done this, having gained a firsthand appreciation for their various skills (it's never as easy as it looks), you will be able to make decisions with a clearer understanding of the implications for the troops and for the broader undertaking. And, as always, if you've gotten down and dirty with your troops and they believe you understand and respect what they do. Then, when the going gets rough and you ask them to take it up a notch, they will not hesitate to rise to the challenge.

It is critical to understand this hypersensitivity about respect when you're a leader trying to get an enterprise to work together to accomplish a goal. This is especially true when you are leading groups across different organizations. What bearing does this have on you as a leader? Individuals (and organizations) carry scars from past humiliations and slights, real or perceived. In today's more interconnected world, you could be leading not just in a narrow organization but across multiple organizations, disciplines, cultures, and so on. If you, as a leader, don't try to know and understand them (note I didn't say necessarily sympathize), you will not be able to manage your interaction with them successfully.

I have certainly found this to be true in the interagency environment in Washington, DC (see chapter 6 on tribalism). I am constantly discovering decades-old interagency scars. Once, the deputy director of a major intelligence agency told me an officer in his organization was cursing a blue streak about those "bastards across the river" (us). With some alarm about yet another brewing flare-up, I quickly asked the deputy when this took place. He said the officer, through very tightly gritted teeth, hissed, "1962!" Our discussion took place in 1995. Like tribal blood feuds in the hills of Afghanistan, which can span many generations, memories of these events are seared deeply into our cultures and passed on religiously from generation to generation as part of tribal lore. New members of the group absorb these lessons, implicitly and explicitly. Your job as a leader is to understand this and develop strategies to increase communication, understanding, and a bit of empathy for the other guy so you can best hope to manage (notice I didn't say solve) these factors.

VISION (ABILITY TO CHART A SUCCESSFUL COURSE OF ACTION)

If you don't know where you're going, you might wind up someplace else.

Yogi Berra,
American philosopher

Vision is another way of describing the ability to assess a strategic challenge and determine a broad course of action with a good chance of accomplishing the given task—the ability to take stock of the situation and see past the short term to what needs to be done for long-term success. An effective leader is able to form such a vision—a road map—of the conditions that need to be established in order to achieve the goals set for her team. I mentioned early on that one of the reasons people need a leader is that there is a difficult job to be done. When faced with such a task, a leader must be able to methodically analyze the situation—to do what engineers call a systems analysis, to insightfully deconstruct the problem into its constituent parts, figure out what's going on, and devise a course of action that will result in efficient and effective accomplishment of the mission.

Former secretary of state Colin Powell offered the following advice for choosing an effective leader:

Look for intelligence and judgment and, most critically, a capacity to anticipate, to see around corners. Also look for loyalty, integrity, a high energy drive, a balanced ego and the drive to get things done.

Once you have determined your course of action, the job is by no means over—quite the contrary. It is equally important—and difficult— to galvanize the workforce to follow your vision, to keep them motivated, to maintain project momentum, and, critically, to be prepared to deal with the unexpected. The nineteenth-century military theorist Carl von Clausewitz had a term for the unexpected: friction, or what others term the fog of war. It comprises those factors—natural and man-made, random and unpredictable—that turn the seemingly simple into the exceedingly difficult, factors that undermine or work against the commander's original battle plan. The term encompasses all those real-world annoyances—internal and external—like faulty intelligence, unreliable communications, weather, and luck that inevitably upset the best-laid plans, to say nothing of enemy commanders who are so inconsiderate as to ignore the planner's preconceptions of their situation, resources, morale, actions, and reactions. In your leadership, you must always be prepared to scramble and adapt to the ever-changing situation. We joke in my directorate that long-term planning for us is scribbling a map on the back of an envelope and agreeing to meet on some dark street three hours later. But not for complex operations. Those require carefully thought-out doctrine and strategy, informed by vision, meticulous planning, and the ability to adjust in the heat of battle.

An important corollary to vision is foresight—the ability to look into the future and anticipate how conditions will evolve, thereby threatening your ability to deliver on your mission, and to devise an effective strategy for dealing with these challenges. Today's world is characterized by rapid, unanticipated change, and the speed and complexity of that change is only going to increase. People who can see these trends coming and build strategies to effectively deal with them are leaders. Such leaders are rare, and they will always be at a premium.

TOLERANCE FOR HONEST MISTAKES

To make no mistakes is not in the power of man; but from their errors and mistakes the wise and good learn wisdom for the future.

Plutarch,
Greek biographer and moralist, AD 46–120

The proper handling of the inevitable mistakes, misfortunes, and flaps is a skill that I believe is critical to effective leadership. In intelligence operations, in business, and in life, we often ask our people to take on tough missions and sometimes put themselves at risk. Too often when these teams, in the thick of action, run into trouble, the establishment (safe and comfortable back at Headquarters, with plenty of time on their hands for Monday-morning quarterbacking) want to set up a board of inquiry and "hold someone accountable." (Of course, when the crisis arrives, and drastic action is required, these same "leaders" wonder why their people are so "risk averse.")

In our Program, we are acutely aware of the old saw, "People who don't make mistakes rarely make anything." If you want to tackle the impossible, you'd better be prepared to accept risk and deal with the inevitable mistakes. Oscar Wilde said, "Experience is simply the name we give our mistakes." And hotel magnate Conrad Hilton, a tremendously successful leader, noted that "success seems to be connected with action. Successful people keep moving. They make mistakes, but they don't quit."

Several years ago, we sent a team out on a mission of crucial importance, where the political consequences of compromise could have been most serious. One of our best officers, working long hours under great stress, made one of the few almost-irretrievable mistakes inside the target building. He managed to recover and get things back in working order and, in the end, there was no compromise. But he returned home with his tail between his legs (our group of type As is highly competitive). I sought him out shook his hand, and, to his surprise, told him we counted him a hero. (He responded that this was a novel reaction.) I explained that he had been using equipment that had been painstakingly certified by our engineering teams. He used the techniques we had similarly certified. And he himself had passed through the training program and been certified to carry out these missions. In the field, something had happened, though it was not clear if it was an equipment malfunction or human error. What was important, though, was that he had followed procedures to the letter, including putting the equipment he had knocked out back in working order in record time. Under great pressure, he had kept his nerve and come through. I told him we could ask no more of him, adding that if we jettisoned every officer who made a mistake there would be plenty of empty spaces in the parking lot, starting with mine. While protecting the officer's identity, I have used this example ever since in talking to our teams before an operation. It is critical for our people to have confidence that if they are going to fix bayonets and close with the enemy on our behalf, and an honest mistake is made, no one is going to be sacrificed in a quest to mollify outside (or inside) critics. Otherwise, we can kiss hard-target operations good-bye.

In his 2015 annual command guidance, Commandant of the Marine Corps Gen. Joseph Dunford recognized this need to accept honest mistakes if young leaders are to be developed. Leaders of all levels must be willing to accept mistakes as part of the learning process:

> *[E]rrors by junior officers stemming from overboldness are a necessary part of learning. We should deal with such errors leniently; there must be no "zero defects" mentality. Abolishing "zero defects" means that we do not stifle boldness or initiative through the threat of punishment. It does not mean that commanders do not counsel subordinates on mistakes; constructive criticism is an important element in learning. Nor does it give subordinates free license to act stupidly or recklessly.*[31]

With this in mind, we have developed and promulgated to our teams what I hope is a crystal-clear policy on mistakes:

- We will ask you to engage in activities where the consequences in the event things go wrong can be most unpleasant—unpleasant for the country, unpleasant for the mission, unpleasant for you.

- If you were acting in good faith, to the best of your ability…if you were working according to the procedures you were trained in…if you were using the equipment as you were trained, and the proverbial stuff hits the fan or you make an honest mistake, *we will back you up.*

---

31 Marine Corps Doctrinal Publication 1,. Department of the Navy, Headquarters United States Marine Corps, Washington, D.C. 1997: 57.

- On the other hand, if there is a failure of *integrity* or *character*... if you think you're smarter than everyone else and try to rewrite or ignore the rules of tradecraft and operational security for your own convenience...if you somehow jeopardize the mission and your fellow team members by irresponsible, immoral, or dishonest behavior, *you can expect to be held duly accountable and face release from the Program.*

You may wish to consider a similar set of guidelines for your "operations."

WORK ETHIC/PERSISTENCE

Every morning in Africa, a gazelle awakens. It knows that it must outrun the fastest lion that day or be eaten. Every morning in Africa, a lion also awakens. It knows that it must outrun the slowest gazelle or starve to death. The moral of the story is this: whether you are a gazelle or a lion, when you wake up, you had better be running.

African folk proverb

Work ethic and persistence are two different but closely related character traits. There are many names for this family of qualities—moxie, grit, relentlessness—but it basically amounts to the same thing: first, you need to work hard; second, you can never give up. You may personify all the leadership qualities enumerated here, but that by no means relieves you of the need to constantly work hard at it. This is not something you do once to win over your troops when you arrive. You must live these principles every day for the rest of your career. Remember: **That which comprises the harshest burden, a king lifts first**

and sets down last. When things get ugly, you'll be tempted to back off. But ask yourself—what will I think of myself if I let my guys down or don't do my duty? What will they think of me if I shirk the hard work and risks? They'll do the same, and…you are *not* a leader.

In *Freedom, Inc.*, their 2009 book on business productivity, coauthors Brian Carney and Isaac Getz write about an entrepreneur named Bob Davids who started and ran numerous businesses throughout a long and successful career. At one of his companies, he would clean the floor himself in order to free up his employees to do more important work. No job was too small if it meant advancing the interests of the company and his workforce. Every rung you step up on the ladder makes these points *more* valid and *increases* the burden you carry on your shoulders. Two of our Program leaders of general-officer rank once literally (and happily) schlepped gravel for twelve hours a day for a week so that a team preparing for the field could concentrate on their specialized, mission-critical training rather than waste precious time shoveling. *That* is leadership, whether you're a king or a leader.

In an book entitled "Talent Is Overrated," Geoff Colvin, senior editor-at-large at *Fortune* magazine, cites facts and research that suggest that the so-called eureka moment is a myth. The greatest innovators in a wide range of fields have all spent many years in intensive preparation before making any kind of creative breakthrough. There seems to be a ten-year rule, even for the top performers, which says that this much time is usually needed before someone is ready to make a creative breakthrough. Years of deliberate practice and hard work are required.[32]

The best of leaders embody this quality of refusing to quit no matter what the odds. When the task is routine and not particularly challenging, average managers can hack it. It is when the going gets rough that *real* leaders are required. The harder, more onerous the problem, the more impossible it looks, the more the top deck will be looking

---

32 Geoff Colvin, "Talent Is Overrated: What Really Separates World-Class Performers from Everybody Else," *Portfolio Trade*, 2010.

for the leader who will stay the course and drive home to success. It is no coincidence that the family motto of Ernest Shackleton, the most famous endurer of modern history, was *fortitudine vincimus*—"by endurance we conquer."

No less a leader than T. E. Lawrence (Lawrence of Arabia) wrote: "All men dream: but not equally. Those who dream by night in the dusty recesses of their minds wake in the day to find that it was vanity: but the dreamers of the day are dangerous men, for they may act out their dream with open eyes, to make it possible."[33] As a leader, be a dreamer of the day; chart your vision, and then pursue it relentlessly.

PASSION

If you aren't fired with enthusiasm, you'll be fired...with enthusiasm.

Vince Lombardi,
legendary coach of the Green Bay Packers, 1959–1967

The really tough jobs cannot be tackled with intellectual power and cold analytic rigor alone. You need passion—a fierce dedication to some goal, some cause, something you deeply believe is worthy of your full effort and devotion. I have found that the one common denominator among all our successful teams—both leaders and troops—is a passion for the mission. Despite pay-for-performance schemes that come in and out of vogue, I have found that few, if any, of the best leaders (or troops, for that matter) are in it for the money. (In fact, we all admit,

---

33 T. E. Lawrence, *Seven Pillars of Wisdom: A Triumph* (London: M. Pike, with the assistance of H. J. Hodgson, 1926).

only half-jokingly, that we would pay to do what we do.) My career-planning advice to those who seek it is: don't obsess over climbing the corporate ladder. Find a cause for which you can't wait to jump out of bed in the morning, wanting to get to the job; few people are so lucky. I think most people would eagerly choose a job they felt passionate about over a job that paid more. I have talked to several businessmen worth billions, and more than one of them enviously said (regrettably only half-jokingly) that he would gladly give it all up for a job that fired the passion the way ours does. (We're still waiting on the paperwork for the exchange.)

In his 1995 study on the principles of special operations, US Navy SEAL Admiral William McRaven noted that "the one constant that prevailed throughout the eight case studies [that framed McRaven's thesis on unconventional operations] was the motivation of the individual soldier." He calls it "purpose…understanding and executing the prime objective of the mission regardless of emerging obstacles or opportunities." He quotes General Joshua Shani, the air commander of the 1976 Israeli hostage rescue at Entebbe airfield, Uganda: "We were absolutely committed to seeing the task completed." Captain Otto Skorzeny, leader of the daring September 1943 rescue of Italian dictator Benito Mussolini, noted, "When a man is moved by pure enthusiasm and by the conviction that he is risking his life in a noble cause…he provides the essential element of success."[34] People who love their jobs are anxious to find better ways to do more, and more creative, work. Don't expect to find much creativity and innovation from "crank-turners," those who just show up and do the same job, day after day, with little imagination or initiative.

It is one of the principal duties of a leader to identify, inculcate, and reinforce that sense of purpose in those he or she leads. It goes without

---

34 William H. McRaven, *Spec Ops—Case Studies in Special Operations Warfare: Theory and Practice* (Novato, CA: Presidio, 1995): 23.

saying that this passion had better be sincere. If yours is not, the troops will know, and...you are *not* a leader.

INITIATIVE

[B]ut when I said that nothing had been done I erred in one important matter. We had definitely committed ourselves and were halfway out of our ruts...This may sound too simple, but is great in consequence. Until one is committed, there is hesitancy, the chance to draw back, always ineffectiveness. Concerning all acts of initiative (and creation), there is one elementary truth, the ignorance of which kills countless ideas and splendid plans: that the moment one definitely commits oneself, then providence moves too. A whole stream of events issues from the decision, raising in one's favor all manner of unforeseen incidents, meetings and material assistance, which no man could have dreamt would have come his way.

William H. Murray,
The Scottish Himalayan Expedition 1951

This particular trait comes under different names, including "initiative" or being "proactive" or a "self-starter." As I said earlier, bosses are always looking for the can-do leader, the officer who can get the job done with minimal supervision. In fact, in our organization one of the greatest compliments you can pay someone in a performance appraisal is, "requires minimal supervision." That means the boss can assign a task and turn back to other pressing business, confident that the job will be accomplished expeditiously and with minimal need for the manager to intrude. Great leaders love this kind of employee, in part because there is nothing more irritating than to be constantly interrupted by your team lead who has a problem and wants you to tell him what to do next. I recall early in my career, still a fairly junior officer, carefully outlining several options for my chief: "On the one hand, we could do this...or, on the other hand, we might do this..." I thought I had done a pretty good analytic job and had neatly laid out the options so he could choose the one he thought best. He looked at me with no little exasperation and said, "No, I pay *you* to tell *me* what to do!" Sure shocked the hell out of me, but the lesson has stayed with me forty years later. Author, web pioneer, and entrepreneur Bo Bennet points out that "without initiative, leaders are simply workers in leadership positions." (More on all this in a later chapter, "What Is Expected of a Leader?")

RELIABILITY

Success in life doesn't depend on how you handle Plan A; it depends on how you handle Plan B.

Larry P—leader,
Former Army Ranger and Program sage

For a leader, ours is a world of great challenges, frequent setbacks, and endless thrash and upheaval. In complex undertakings, the leader is simultaneously moving multiple pieces around the chessboard, ideally considering many moves ahead. As teams move into action, the leader will deploy additional pieces on the assumption that the pieces moved earlier are carrying out their instructions as ordered. There is a fine line between your troops taking initiative in the face of changed circumstances and chucking the plan out the window because they "know better" or simply felt like doing something else.

But at the end of the day, you will rely on this discipline to maximize your chances of success. Whether you are leading or being led, your fellows must be able to rely on you doing your job the way it was laid out. The same holds true for the information you report: the plan is constantly evolving as more information flows in from various business units. If reporting is not reliable, even the best plans will unravel. Your status reporting and that of those reporting to you *must* be reliable.

As in most things, the ancient Greeks can serve as a lesson in reliability. The phalanx was a military formation made up of heavy infantry, or hoplites, armed with spears. A hoplite's shield would cover his own left side and overlap to protect the right side of the man to his left, each one necessarily relying on his comrade to protect his flank. In this way, a solid wall of shields created a nearly impenetrable front while the hoplites ground forward, driving their spears against the enemy. The effectiveness of the phalanx was entirely dependent on the discipline of the warriors. If they maintained the integrity of the formation, victory was all but assured; if the formation broke, all was lost. *Everything—victory, life itself—depended on the steadfastness and courage of the man who fought alongside.*

This is no less true 2,500 years later, and not just on the field of battle. It's equally true in every arena of human competition and conflict. They're counting on you, trusting they can rely on you. Your boss needs to know he or she can count on you to carry out your instructions; your team needs to know you will have their backs.

MATURITY

A mature person is one who does not think only in absolutes, who is able to be objective even when deeply stirred emotionally, who has learned that there is both good and bad in all people and all things, and who walks humbly and deals charitably.

Eleanor Roosevelt

As a leader, you will be handed grave responsibilities—for mission, for resources, for your company's success, perhaps even for people's lives. Maturity means putting mission before self. Maturity means standing up for what you believe, however menacingly the crowd jeers. Maturity means taking the long view, understanding that what matters in life is what you do for others—what you leave behind as a legacy, not what publicity you can garner today or what riches you can accrue. Maturity means being able to recognize in oneself the human frailties of emotion, envy, avarice, lust for revenge, and insecurity, and being able, day after day, to discipline and control them, to rise above them—most significantly, when no one else is looking. This really counts when the going gets tough, when you face adversity…when, alone, you must stand in the face of the storm for what you believe.

In order to do the job, a leader must exercise power, but exercise it judiciously. The Greeks had a word for the outrageous abuse of power—"hubris." Lord Acton probably wasn't the first to point out that power corrupts and absolute power corrupts absolutely. A leader holds off this corruption through the exercise of humility and selflessness. With maturity acquired through age, experience, and integrity, reinforced by discipline, you can step up to the task, lead, and see the job through to the end. A Naval Academy colleague tells me he once heard the highly decorated and deeply respected General James Mattis, commander of the First Marine Division during the 2003 invasion of Iraq, respond to a question from a well-meaning civilian: "Sir, how can we [civilians] help you with the *burden* you and our forces have endured in this time of war?" General Mattis responded, "I think 'burden' is an unfortunate choice of words. It has been my *privilege* to serve in this way…I feel blessed to have done so." (Emphases mine.)

JUDGMENT

It is not by muscle, speed, or physical dexterity that great things are achieved, but by reflection, force of character, and judgment.

Marcus Tullius Cicero,
Roman statesman, author, and orator (106–43 BC)

The Roman historian Tacitus, who was a student of leadership, wrote that reason and calm judgments were the qualities especially belonging to a leader. Judgment is about making decisions, and that's what a leader is expected to do. Something needs to be done. Some course needs to be set. This requires decisions, which had better be the right ones. How do you make these decisions? After all, it's easy to say "exercise good judgment," but it's another thing entirely to work out which course of action is the "good" one. A lot of it comes down to native intelligence and experience. In the objective sense, you call on these and all other aspects of your character and experience. But the more subjective challenge is to establish priorities, keeping a clear focus on what is important and weighing (judging) what is the proper thing to do at that particular time and in that particular situation. You think about what is right (for the greater good, not for yourself), what is best for your troops, what is moral, what is ethical.

I don't think there is any way to teach judgment, although you can help out along the way. It is something that must come from within, from your own experience, from observing other leaders—good and bad—over time and learning from those observations. As Nietzsche might have said, what doesn't kill you will leave you with stronger judgment. The development of good judgment is an ongoing process, not an instantaneous or episodic one. You will constantly be making multiple decisions over long periods of time—some good, some bad. The Greeks would tell you that the gods are watching, testing your mettle, seeing what you're made of, ever alert to signs of hubris. Are your decisions made in favor of your own interest? Or do you make them in the interest of the greater good?

DECISIVENESS

The mind of Caesar. It is the reverse of most men's. It rejoices in committing itself. To us arrive each day a score of challenges; we must say yes or no to decisions that will set off chains of consequences. Some of us deliberate; some of us refuse the decision, which is itself a decision; some of us leap giddily into the decision, setting our jaws and closing our eyes, which is the sort of decision of despair. Caesar embraces decision. It is as though he felt his mind to be operating only when it is interlocking itself with significant consequences. Caesar shrinks from no responsibility.

Thornton Wilder, American novelist and playwright
The Ides of March

Whenever one thinks about leadership, the descriptor "decisive" immediately comes to mind. After all, what does leadership consist of but making decisions? It is often said that any decision is better than no decision at all, and that's probably true in most cases. Theodore Roosevelt is credited with writing, "In any moment of decision the best thing you can do is the right thing, the next best thing is the wrong thing, and the worst thing you can do is nothing." In terms of leadership, whether the observer is your boss or someone who works for you, the expectation is that some course of action will be selected, and action will ensue. If you can't make timely decisions, you can't be a leader, and no one will follow. In effect, decision making is the very essence of being a leader.

Of course, it's not enough by itself to just make decisions; your decisions had better be informed by the other traits listed above, ensuring they are consistent with your standards of integrity and justice, maturely weighed, with full consideration for the first- and second-order effects of your actions. You will be accountable and, more importantly, must live with the consequences. Unfortunately, there is no silver bullet, no secret algorithm that will inevitably guide you to the right decision. That's why being a leader requires courage. Again, here's Teddy Roosevelt, this time from *The Strenuous Life*: "Far better it is to dare mighty things, to win glorious triumphs, even though checkered by failure, than to take rank with those poor spirits who neither enjoy much nor suffer much, because they live in the gray twilight that knows not victory nor defeat."[35]

But decide you must. Here's President Harry Truman reflecting in August 1945 on his decision to approve the dropping of the atomic bomb on Hiroshima:

I realize the tragic significance of the atomic bomb…It is an awful responsibility which has come to us…We thank God that it has come to us, instead of to our enemies; and we pray that He may guide us to use it in His ways and for His purposes.[36]

Hopefully your decisions will not rise to the level of launching a nuclear strike, but you can take it to the bank that you will face hard

---

35 Theodore Roosevelt (1858–1919). The Strenuous Life. Speech before the Hamilton Club, Chicago, April 10, 1899

36 Harry S. Truman, *A Report to the American People on the Potsdam Conference*, radio address from the White House, August 9, 1945

decisions that will profoundly affect people's lives, livelihoods, and the success of your undertaking, in Thornton Wilder's very apt phrase, "interlocking itself with significant consequences." It's one of the fundamental realities of leadership.

Chapter 4

WHAT IS EXPECTED OF
A LEADER?

*In appreciation for whatever it is that makes men accomplish
the impossible.*

Alfred Lansing,
Dedication from *Endurance: Shackleton's Incredible Voyage*

Obviously, many things are to be expected of a leader. But, in those really tough situations when a leader in the true sense of the word is desperately needed, just what is it that those in charge and those being led are looking for? To that end, I would again go back to the essential concept that your job as a leader is to be an effective solver of tough problems, and I would reiterate that the need for dynamic leadership is directly proportional to the importance of the goal and the intractability of the challenge. The tougher the going, the greater the need for great leadership. Moreover, at the end of the day, it's results that matter, be it in a hospital operating room, a military campaign, the corporate boardroom, the athletic field, the halls of academia—or leading the country to life, liberty, and the pursuit of happiness. Arguably the single most important contribution a leader can make is what the first President Bush referred to as "the vision thing," seeing what no one has seen before and then making it happen. Instances of this abound through history, across all cultures and ages. In the following pages, I'll talk about some of these historical examples to illustrate what great leaders of the past have done to change the game and how you can take their actions as a guide for your own leadership. Not surprisingly, these stories will also illuminate many of the leadership traits described earlier, such as courage, rigorous analysis, integrity, persistence in the face of opposition, and passion.

The polar opposite of the type of visionary leader I'm advocating, the kind unfortunately too often encountered today, is the "crank turner," mentioned earlier. He's the one who's content to run the same plays every Sunday. You hire him, assign him a task, and he works at it diligently enough, but he never seems to summon the imagination to think about how he might do it better. The chassis rolls by him on the assembly line, and he dutifully bolts on the next part, never stopping to ask if there is a better way to skin that particular cat. That astute chronicler of human nature, Rudyard Kipling, had his number when he wrote: "In most big undertakings, one or two men do the work while the rest sit near and talk till the ripe decorations begin to fall."[37] Those are the guys who always make themselves scarce until the medals start being handed out—the very antithesis of a leader.

In contrast to the innovative, proactive leader, the essayist William Deresiewicz described a different sort of bureaucrat in a 2009 address to plebes at West Point, drawing from Joseph Conrad's novel of Africa, *Heart of Darkness.* Conrad's protagonist Marlow has been sent up the Congo River by a shipping company to retrieve one of their managers who's gone rogue. (The movie *Apocalypse Now* was based on the book.)

---

37 Rudyard Kipling, "Wressley of the Foreign Office," in *Plain Tales from the Hills* (New York: John W. Lovell, 1889).

At one of his stops, the Central Station, Marlow describes the station manager, the kind Deresiewicz says tends to prosper in the bureaucratic environment: "He was obeyed, yet he inspired neither love nor fear, nor even respect…. He had no genius for organizing, for initiative, or for order…. He had no learning, and no intelligence. His position had come to him—why?... he could keep the routine going—that's all."[38]

That is, just "turning the crank," with no questions asked or curiosity aroused. Deresiewicz then asks why it is so often that the best people are stuck in the middle and the leaders are the mediocrities, adding that "excellence isn't usually what gets you up the greasy pole. What gets you up is a talent for maneuvering. Kissing up to the people above you, kicking down to the people below you…picking a powerful mentor and riding his coattails until it's time to stab him in the back…Just keep the routine going."[39] Maybe true in a lot of places, but not where—to borrow an old buzzword—a paradigm shift is critical to mission success.

In truth, many employers don't really encourage their employees to think. And for some employees, in some jobs, that may be just what you want. *But not in a leader.* What senior officials, at least those who are themselves good leaders, are really looking for in their leaders—what they *expect* from their leaders—is someone who is *not* satisfied with the status quo, someone who is always asking, "Why do we do it this way?"; someone who always believes there *must* be a better way and gets down on his knees and pans the creek until he finds gold. Admittedly, this type can sometimes drive you crazy, and they certainly make a lot of people—above, below, and alongside them in the organization—feel nervous, sometimes threatened. There are several such "deliverers" in our Program that I have to follow around with a pooper-scooper, sweeping up broken crockery, owing to their less-than-stellar interpersonal skills. But in their case, it's more than worth it because they deliver. For the

---

38 Joseph Conrad, *Heart of Darkness* (New Jersey, J.P.Piper Books, 2015)

39 William Deresiewicz, "Solitude and Leadership," 2009, https://theamericanscholar.org/solitude-and-leadership/.

intractable challenges we face, those that most judge to be impossible, the organization needs people with the initiative, drive, and persistence to find a better way to lead their teams to mission accomplishment. A little broken crockery is a small price to pay.

The leader, then, is expected not to be a crank turner, but to be the generator of solutions to the organization's toughest problems—the one who can be counted on to get the ball across the goal line. Let's look at some examples.

THE FOUNDING FATHERS

Talk about leadership! The American Revolution saw perhaps the most fortunate confluence of great leaders in history, unusual in their wisdom, patriotism, selflessness, integrity, and character and, significantly, their understanding of the lessons of history. We owe the freedoms we enjoy today to the vision and leadership of these statesmen, George Washington first among them. Our Founding Fathers led in every sense of the word. Against all odds, they overcame the most powerful military force of their time and went on to establish the foundations for the greatest country that has ever graced the earth, a beacon of liberty and opportunity. Broadly educated—some more through self-study than formal—and deeply committed to the ideals of the rights of man, they embodied all those traits we hope to see in our leaders. They embodied integrity. They possessed the courage to pledge to each other their lives, their fortunes, their sacred honor. They were masters of rhetoric, both written and spoken. Their words inspired a new country, the first ever founded on a principle rather than on geography, ethnicity, or military might. They saw what was—British colonial rule; and then saw what could be—a new country...a country, as Abraham Lincoln would so eloquently phrase it at Gettysburg, conceived in liberty and dedicated to the proposition that all men are created equal.

At the end of the Revolutionary War, George Washington wanted nothing more than to return to his farm in northern Virginia. But, as postwar turmoil continued, one of his officers sent him a letter arguing that democracy could never survive and urging Washington to don the mantel of king. The general, a patriot of the highest order, was deeply offended and insisted that his men never again entertain such an idea. He responded:

Sir: With a mixture of great surprise and astonishment I have read with attention the Sentiments you have submitted to my perusal. Be assured Sir, no occurrence in the course of the War, has given me more painful sensations than your information of there being such ideas existing in the Army as you have expressed, and I must view with abhorrence, and reprehend with severety…

I am much at a loss to conceive what part of my conduct could have given encouragement to an address which to me seems big with the greatest mischiefs that can befall my Country. If I am not deceived in the knowledge of myself, you could not have found a person to whom your schemes are more disagreeable…. Let me conjure you then, if you have any regard for your Country, concern for yourself or posterity, or respect for me, to banish these thoughts from your Mind, and never communicate, as from yourself, or any one else, a sentiment of the like Nature.[40]

With the idea of kingship dismissed, Washington continued to deflect the suggestion that he should take a leadership role of any sort in the new government. In the end, though, he was prevailed on to continue his service for the good of the country. Then, after two terms, in defiance of millennia of historical precedent, Washington gracefully stood aside and retired to civilian life. Two centuries later, he is still seen as the gold standard of American leadership. Washington shared

---

40 Letter from Washington to Lewis Nicola, May 22, 1782, George Washington Papers, 1741–1799: Series 4, General Correspondence, 1697–1799, Manuscript Division, Library of Congress, Washington, DC.

with our other Founding Fathers a vision of what could be—not a better monarchy, just with fairer taxes and representation for the colonies, but a fundamentally new concept of self-government, a nation devoted to the idea that all men are created equal, endowed by their Creator with certain unalienable rights, and that governments derive their powers from the consent of the governed.

"WILD BILL" DONOVAN AND THE OSS

We can take another lesson from the history of American intelligence: going into World War II, Medal of Honor recipient William "Wild Bill" Donovan understood the need for an organization to collect and analyze information to inform the decisions of policy makers and military leaders (even if many of them vehemently disagreed with the proposition). As described in a biography by Douglas Waller, in the face of prolonged and fierce opposition, Donovan

> created a large and far-flung intelligence operation while fighting a war at the same time.... The institutional and cultural resistance he faced from the national security establishment of his day was exceptional.... [S]o foreign were Donovan's concepts for intelligence and unconventional warfare to the prevailing military and political mind-set, his intramural battles took on an added ferocity.... [H]e was spending as much time fighting his allies as he did the enemy.... The agency Donovan created would send an organizational theorist into convulsion. It became a Rube Goldberg collection of disparate programs, functions, and initiatives.... By any measure, he was a bad manager.... [P] ractically all [his men] praised him as a remarkable leader... Without Donovan's creativity, his charisma, his intelligence, his open-mindedness, his personal courage, and his vision for the future, an unconventional organization like the OSS would likely not have been organized or sustained throughout the war...

*Donovan and his men began their work as rank amateurs...
but as the war progressed they improved...The daring, the risk
taking, the unconventional thinking, the élan and esprit de corps
of the OSS would permeate the new agency...Donovan...was
one of the men who shaped modern warfare.*[41]

Donovan's legacy lives on in the Central Intelligence Agency, established as a new organization after World War II to provide intelligence independent of government departments that might want it spun to suit their programmatic, policy, and budgetary ends. Donovan's vision and refusal to bend to the entrenched bureaucracy provided the concept, organization, and, perhaps most importantly, the dogged persistence drive to bring the new agency into existence.

PRISONERS OF WAR

In *Leading with Honor*, a wonderful book about lessons in leadership he took from his experience as a prisoner of war in Vietnam, former US Air Force pilot Lee Ellis convincingly illustrates the critical importance of good leadership in the most stressful situations. In this must-read for all aspiring leaders, Ellis tells stories of remarkable courage in what must be one of the harshest crucibles of leadership imaginable. He makes the case that brutal environments such as a POW camp teach valuable lessons of leadership—good and bad—in the starkest terms. Our POWs in Vietnam lived up to the highest standards of our military and national values, taking strength by not allowing their captors to undermine their solidarity and resistance. Ellis details how POWs kept faith with each other, their values, and their country, sharing meager rations and tending to their sick and badly injured comrades in the face of the worst the Vietnamese could dish out. Particularly early in the

---

41 Douglas Waller, *Wild Bill Donovan: The Spymaster Who Created the OSS and Modern American Espionage* (New York: Free Press, 2011).

war, the POWs were subjected to extensive torture, with the aim of breaking their will in order to enlist them in propaganda efforts meant to characterize American military actions as war crimes. Eventually, after long and horrific episodes of torture, most POWs—many of them in prison for six or more years—would crack and make some concession to their captors. Given the military Code of Conduct that these brave Americans were sworn to live by, they returned to their cells, crushed by the shame they felt at giving in. Recognizing that no individual can hold out forever against such torture, the senior officers (leaders) developed a concept they called "bouncing back," which meant that each prisoner should hold out as long as he could and, beyond that, give away as little as possible. When he returned to the general population, his fellows tended not just to his physical injuries but, equally importantly, to his spiritual needs, helping restore his dignity and sense of honor. It has to be one of the greatest examples of collective courage in history, and *it could only have happened under the most determined and exemplary of leaders.*

The Vietnamese tried offering early release to prisoners who cooperated. To their ever-lasting credit, the POWs agreed among themselves that, if given the opportunity for release, they would only agree to go in order of capture, those taken earliest being first to go. A young naval aviator, Lieutenant Commander (now Senator) John McCain, was shot down over North Vietnam in October 1967. During ejection, he suffered extensive injuries, which were compounded by mistreatment when he was captured. His right arm was broken in three places, and he was bayoneted and suffered brutal blows to the head. Realizing that McCain's father, Admiral John S. McCain, was not just a senior naval officer, but as Commander in Chief of the Pacific Command—overall commander of US forces in the war—the North Vietnamese smelled a propaganda coup if they could arrange to release him on "humanitarian grounds." McCain, by his own admission afraid, sick, and still suffering greatly from his wounds, badly wanted to accept release. But his integrity, courage, and the rock-solid system of leadership by the senior officers in the camp enabled him to maintain his resolve:

[McCain] could easily have justified his decision [to go home]. Instead, he confronted his doubts and fears with his commitments to the honor of his family and the service of his country and fellow POWs. He would refuse early release.... [The Vietnamese political boss at the camp] continued to pressure McCain, even telling him that President Johnson had ordered him to come home. John...[made] it clear that he would have nothing of it. He gave his final answer...in a voice loud enough for fellow POWs in nearby cells to overhear.... His actions sent a message that came through loud and clear... "I will return with honor." [42]

Ellis' book is a great read for the young leader, illuminating in the starkest terms the critical nature of *in extremis* leadership. The leader is expected to see what needs to be done, however onerous the circumstances, and summon the moral strength to do what is right.

ACADEMIA

A friend who is an English professor was recently called in to review the curriculum in a university's graduate program. At some length, the faculty detailed to her the problem they were trying to solve with the new curriculum. However, instead of simply accepting that proposition, she questioned and deconstructed it, only to discover that the problem was not the curriculum. In fact, the faculty leadership had incorrectly diagnosed the problem. Had she not taken a step back and examined the basic premises of the task, she would have ended up wasting a lot of time working on the wrong problem. In the end, she was able to put

---

42 Lee Ellis, *Leading with Honor: Leadership Lessons from the Hanoi Hilton* (Cumming, GA: FreedomStar Media, 2012): 50.

the faculty on the road to addressing their real deficiencies. There is a danger in unquestioning acceptance of the conventional wisdom or the other guy's assessment of what's actually afoot.

STEVE JOBS

In terms of what is expected of a leader, I have repeatedly stressed that the effective leader can't just accept the status quo. A great example of leading in this sense (tackling the hard problems, coming up with innovative solutions, and not just accepting "this is the way we have always done it") is the late Steve Jobs. One of the most effective innovators and turnaround artists of modern times, Jobs made Apple into the world's most valuable company. While he could be hard on those who were unable to keep up with his light-speed pace or would not match his work ethic or fanatical attention to detail, he was a strategic thinker in the truest sense of the word. He embodied many of the leadership traits discussed above, including the ability to form a vision about how to solve a tough problem and the capability to lead others through successful implementation of that vision. It would be an understatement to say Jobs had passion. Despite some major setbacks, including being exiled from Apple in 1985, Jobs returned in 1997 and, grabbing the struggling company by the scruff of its neck, set it on a course to market dominance. He almost single-handedly staged a revolution that spanned personal computers, animated movies, and the "iFamily" of personal electronic devices—to say nothing of standing the music industry on its head. He had that essential ability we look for in a great leader—to see the problem in a new way. He was able to see beyond portable CD players and the Sony Walkman, to imagine miniature digital devices capable of carrying massive libraries of music, books, and other entertainment—something we take for granted today but a revolution others in the industry not only didn't foresee, *they vigorously resisted it*. To do it, Jobs had to overcome opposition within Apple to many of his visionary ideas. People thought what he was asking was impossible. A good example of this resistance to change is the so-called GUI ("gooey"), the graphical user interface—that almost-universal system by which you today control your computer by clicking your mouse on icons. Jobs noted:

> *We fought tooth and nail with a variety of people there who thought the whole concept of a graphical user interface was crazy...on the grounds that it couldn't be done, or on the grounds that real computer users didn't need menus in plain English.... But fortunately, I was the largest stockholder and the chairman of the company, so I won.*[43]

Jobs was bold in his vision, relentless in execution, meticulous in attention to detail, and a leader whose influence on American industry and culture was immeasurable. So if you're going to be the Steve Jobs of your particular organization, how would you approach it? Think about how you would analyze your problem, deconstruct it, and craft a solution that no one else could see, setting your organization on the road to success. How would you face the "tooth and nail" opposition and carry the day? *This* is what is expected of a leader.

LESSONS OF WAR

In his classic military study *Strategy*, the eminent British military historian Sir B. H. Liddell Hart severely criticized generals of World War I who, despite experiencing staggering losses, clung stubbornly to the old Napoleonic strategy of massive frontal assault. However effective it may have been before the introduction of the rifled-bore firearm, it was nothing less than suicidal by the early twentieth century, and it led to the catastrophic casualties of brutal trench warfare—for little gain. A whole generation of Europe's best were sacrificed to this

---

43 "Steve Jobs: 'Computer Science Is a Liberal Art,'" interview by Terry Gross, *Fresh Air* on National Public Radio, February 22, 1996, http://www.npr.org/2011/10/06/141115121/steve-jobs-computer-science-is-a-liberal-art.

folly. Hart argued for the "indirect" attack, which required thinking about the mission, the terrain, and the adversary's capabilities and then devising a plan of maneuver, speed, and surprise to defeat the enemy with minimum effort and casualties (lessons known to Sun Tzu, Alexander of Macedon, Hannibal, Genghis Khan, William Tecumseh Sherman, and many other eminent generals throughout history, but inexplicably lost by the early twentieth century). How does this apply to your performance as a leader? Generals (leaders) who keep doing the same thing over and over again are doomed to failure. The effective leader needs to learn "operational analysis." Don't just study textbooks and blindly apply the techniques therein without first determining their applicability to the particular situation. Study the problem, extrapolate from the professional principles you have learned, and craft your visionary strategy accordingly.

ON THE STREET

Early in my own career, I personally learned this lesson about "operational analysis," vice blindly applying what I had been taught in the classroom. Preparing for an overseas assignment, I attended a rigorous course designed to prepare us to operate in the face of very aggressive and effective opposition. The course was likened to Marine boot camp: tremendous pressure, much more work than time allowed, and monkey wrenches dropped into your plans at the worst possible time. The manual on the applicable tradecraft was referred to as "The Bible." In it were diagrams of routes, street configurations, and tactics that we would employ on the street to avoid detection by the opposition. The training took place on the streets of major American cities, and we trainees were consistently able to use the terrain, intersections, building layouts, and the like to do just about anything we wanted without being detected. The problem was, once we were in the field, it took but a few weeks to realize that our training was irrelevant to the situation we faced. The streets were different, the stores were different, and, clearly, the opposition had not read our manual and insisted in being where they shouldn't be, in a position to see what they shouldn't see. My reaction and that of my fellow officers was the same—we were confused and not a little intimidated. But we quickly banded together and rewrote the book. We developed a custom variant on "The Bible" that fit our particular environment and circumstances. We had learned a critical lesson—*there is no cookie-cutter approach to solving tough problems.* Rather than teach your team *what* to do, better to equip them with the general principles—the *how* to do. They can then work out the optimal, customized solution for that particular situation.

Military commanders don't just locate the enemy and attack as prescribed in the field manual; they consider the mission, the terrain, and the capabilities of the opposing force. They devise strategies and tactics custom tailored to their combat environment. A football team doesn't just show up and run plays sequentially out of the playbook. The offensive coordinator notes where the teams are on the field, the score, and how much time is left on the clock. He factors in what he knows of the strengths and weaknesses of both teams and then sends in the play best suited to that particular moment in the game.

In the same way, the leader doesn't just blindly apply principles or checklists from some leadership book. He or she studies the task assigned, the resources available, and the forces working against success and then crafts a strategic plan accordingly. After that, it's all hard work, persistence, flexibility, and adaptability. This is what worked for leaders from Alexander the Great to Hannibal to Steve Jobs, and it will work for you.

IMPATIENCE AND MOMENTUM

These are just a few examples, from a variety of professions, of how leaders were able to tease out the underlying causes of the problem and get things turned around. Beyond this, though, there are a few other things we should expect in our great leaders. The leader needs to focus on what is important, which is not necessarily what everyone else has thought important in the past. The premises of the strategy must be constantly reexamined and tested. Secondly, at times leaders must *not* be patient. As a leader, you don't get paid to be patient. I will often intentionally set goals that seem impossible and press the team relentlessly. If I give them three months, they will take three months (if not five). So instead, I'll tell them I need it in three weeks. There's a lot of wailing and gnashing of teeth, but more often than not, they make it in under the wire.

Equally challenging for a leader is maintaining momentum. Projects are too often plagued by what I call "dead air"—that is, they take three years to complete, but in reality there's about nine months of actual activity, with the other twenty-seven months burned up in studies...so-and-so is on annual leave...we can't analyze the data because it's being sent by slow boat, and it won't be here for four weeks...and on and on. One of the most important (and most difficult) jobs of the leader, whether in business, the military, academia, or medicine, is to keep up the "operational" momentum. People and teams can do a lot more than they think they can, and the leader's job is to convince them of that.

FAILURE OF IMAGINATION

Organizations, mine included, are too often the victims of failure of imagination. This can hobble an organization fatally in that there are no new ideas to implement and, therefore, no progress. The leader must constantly agitate, refuse to accept conventional wisdom and, with the courage of her convictions, conceive a course of action and muscle it through the opposition. Be careful of so-called best practices; unquestioning acceptance of them can actually put a ceiling on things and discourage innovation.

Writer Walter Isaacson tells the story of the time Steve Jobs marched into the office of Larry Kenyon, the engineer who was working on the

Macintosh operating system, and complained that it was taking too long to boot up:

Kenyon started to explain why reducing the boot-up time wasn't possible, but Jobs cut him off. "If it would save a person's life, could you find a way to shave 10 seconds off the boot time?" he asked. Kenyon allowed that he probably could. Jobs went to a whiteboard and showed that if five million people were using the Mac and it took 10 seconds extra to turn it on every day, that added up to 300 million or so hours a year—the equivalent of at least 100 lifetimes a year. After a few weeks Kenyon had the machine booting up 28 seconds faster.[44]

On the whiteboard in my office, I have a wonderful quote, attributed to the automobile pioneer Henry Ford, that speaks directly to this concept: "If I had asked my customers what they wanted, they would have said a faster horse." In researching the authenticity of this quote, I found a reference on the website QuoteInvestigator.com. While their bottom line is that the quote is probably apocryphal, whether Ford actually said it is less relevant than the fact that it perfectly reflects his philosophy and entrepreneurial instincts.

What all these examples have in common is that the leader was not satisfied with the status quo. Don't let someone else set limits on what you can do. As a leader, be very careful what you let be labeled impossible...*it will prove to be so for that reason, if no other.*

Think about these three approaches to tackling a problem:

1. Receive the tasking, accept it at face value, and figure out how to solve the problem.

---

44 Walter Isaacson, "The Real Leadership Lessons of Steve Jobs," *Harvard Business Review,* April 1, 2012, https://hbr.org/2012/04/the-real-leadership-lessons-of-steve-jobs.

2. Receive the tasking, accept it at face value, and figure out an innovative way to solve the problem.

3. Come up with an entirely new way to look at the problem, examine and redefine how your particular tasking fits into the larger picture, identify an entirely new way to conceive the problem, and then set about solving it.

RESISTANCE AND THE NAY-SAYERS

As a leader, not only must you harness your vision and summon your energy to tackle the mission, you must also be prepared to deal with resistance from any and all quarters. There's a reason "Not invented here!" is one of the most widely used phrases in business. There's something in the human condition that breeds complacency and acceptance of the status quo. The antibodies become particularly aggressive when ideas (or what is perceived as criticism of "the way it's done here") come in from the outside. Libraries of books have been written dealing with how to introduce change into organizations. As far back as the Renaissance, Niccolò Machiavelli warned in his classic treatise on power, *The Prince*, that

> *It must be considered that there is nothing more difficult to carry out, nor more doubtful of success, nor more dangerous to handle, than to initiate a new order of things. For the reformer has enemies in all those who profit by the old order, and only lukewarm defenders in all those who would profit by the new order...because mankind does not truly believe in anything new until they have had actual experience of it.*[45]

---

45 Niccolò Machiavelli, *The Prince* (New York: Bantam, 1984).

And Alexander Hamilton in 1788 was not far behind him: "Men often oppose a thing merely because they had no agency in planning it or because it may have been planned by those whom they dislike."[46]

It's a natural human reaction: if you propose an idea to another group, by definition that means they didn't think of it, which implies they're not on the ball and need you to tell them how to do their business. They may believe that accepting your idea is an admission that they weren't smart enough to think of it. You have to learn how to work with this and get your ideas past this bureaucratic Maginot Line.

RESILIENCE

However good your plan, however skilled your team, however bold your vision, you can expect—as the military saying goes—for the plan to fall apart with the first shot fired. The key to success is flexibility and adaptability. You need to train yourself and your team to deal with an ever-changing "battlefield." Remember Churchill: never quit. Don't expect it to be easy. No one ever wins a basketball game 105–0. Expect to take some hits. The old cliché has it right: it doesn't matter that you get knocked down; what matters is what you do after you get knocked down. If the boss gave you a tough assignment and you encounter problems, what is expected of you—to give up, or to roll with the punches and keep moving on to mission success? A leader knows the answer.

* * *

So what is expected of a leader? A leader is not to be a crank turner, but a "solver of tough [your profession] problems"—someone to whom they can hand over a really tough problem; someone they know will tackle it aggressively, relentlessly, and imaginatively; someone who will be able to draw on a diverse set of experiences and learning; someone

---

46 Alexander Hamilton, "The Executive Department Further Considered," Federalist Paper No. 70, March 15, 1788.

who will not accept the status quo; someone who will not just start by charging directly at the problem, but can (à la Steve Jobs) reexamine the problem in a fundamental way. A leader is a self-starter—someone who will not back down in the face of the fiercest opposition; someone who will approach the job with personal and professional integrity; someone who is willing to be accountable for her decisions and her actions.

Be that leader!

Chapter 5

BECOMING A LEADER

The Greeks believed that character was formed in part by fate and in part by parental training, and that character was exemplified not only by acts of bravery in battle but in the habits of daily conduct.

James Cannon, *Character above All*

NATURE OR NURTURE

So now to the question of how *you* become a leader, which brings us back to the question of whether leaders are born or made. According to BusinessDictionary.com, "Leadership, unlike management, flows from the core of a personality and *cannot be taught, although it may be learnt and may be enhanced through coaching or mentoring*"[47] [emphasis mine]. Even if I could somehow understand this statement (if I could divine how leadership can be learned through coaching and mentoring if

---

47 Businessdictionary.com. http://www.businessdictionary.com/definition/leadership.html. accessed September 15, 2014.

it's not teachable), I don't think I would agree with it. Perhaps they mean the school of hard knocks is the best teacher, vice hiring an Aristotle as a tutor.

A new perspective on the question of building leaders occurred to me recently when I attended a lecture by the aforementioned Colonel Thomas Kolditz of West Point. It helped crystallize some points about leadership that we have been discussing for some years in our Program. It occurred to me that, as in many of today's cultural debates, "nature vs. nurture" is the wrong question. It seems reasonable to assume that leaders are neither purely born nor purely nurtured. It's probably more of a two-part process—part what you bring to the problem and part how you and your mentors mold, refine, develop, and polish that raw material.

There is no question in my mind that, if you aspire to be a leader, then there are certain prerequisites that you either bring to the problem or you don't, without which you cannot excel as a leader. Among them are:

- Integrity, both professional and personal

- Character

- Dedication

- Determination

Show up without them, and no amount of training will get you there. But if you do show up to boot camp with these building blocks, mentors can start to help you to become more conscious of them and to develop your professional skills while you hone your character.

I was challenged on this nature/nurture question in a recent leadership forum, so let me qualify. I am not saying you have to emerge from the womb with rock-solid integrity or you're lost. I'm arguing that you need to show up with these qualities when you report for leadership duty. So, yes, I do believe in redemption; we sinners are salvageable if we set the right course. What I am saying is that, whenever it might be that you do acquire it, it had better be before you assume a position of critical leadership, or it's going to be a very difficult endeavor all around. And don't get hung up on perfection; none of us is perfect. I just mean that you need to be well on the right side of the bell curve of integrity if you are to earn the title of leader. Getting there and staying there takes considerable dedication and psychic energy—hard work, as usual.

There's been a lot published recently about how innate talent is overrated. Daniel Coyle argues in *The Talent Code* that greatness isn't born—it's grown. Researchers today are challenging the idea that innate talent accounts for success at the elite level. Instead, it is more attributable to long and deliberate practice—not traditional practice, but what Coyle terms "deep practice."[48] They advocate good old sweat and hard work. Your accomplishments are essentially a product of the amount of *quality* time you spend working at it. So it is with leadership. If you arrive with the right stuff (character and ability), commit yourself to hard work, maintain the necessary standards of excellence, and adopt the proper attitudes and values, then there is no reason you can't be at least a good leader, if not a great one.

A similar philosophy is articulated in a 2008 article in *Fortune* magazine by senior editor Geoff Colvin. He asks the question: Do you need talent to be successful? Like Coyle, he mounts a pretty convincing argument that innate talent, if in fact there is such a thing, actually has little to do with leadership and career accomplishment. He writes, "We all tend to assume that business giants must possess some special gift for what they do." But, no, a lot of the research on that question seems to indicate that innate talent may be irrelevant. He cites examples across the spectrum, from "Jeffrey Immelt and Steve Balmer who, before age fifty would become CEOs of two of the world's most valuable corporations General Electric…and Microsoft." Looking at their early careers at Proctor and Gamble, no one would have thought these men were

---

48 Daniel Coyle, *The Talent Code: Greatness Isn't Born. It's Grown. Here's How* (New York: Bantam, 2009).

destined to such greatness. Colvin's answer, which we should all take to heart, is that such greatness is achieved largely by what he calls "deliberate practice"—Coyle's "deep practice" ... not just blind hard work, but hard work focused through deliberate and calculated practice. The great performers succeed by "intensely applying this principle...[They] isolate remarkably specific aspects of what they do and focus on those things until they're improved."[49]

So in your development as a leader, don't get hung up on the question of whether you were "born with it." Whatever it is you *were* born with, buttress it with discipline, practice integrity, and then put more work into perfecting it than anyone around you. Average genes and hard work beats great genes and a philosophy of just getting by every time.

THE SECRET SAUCE OF LEADERSHIP?

Leadership is a long business, a tough business, a business where you have to work hard to learn your craft, and you can expect to make plenty of mistakes along the way. A surprising amount of leadership (and life) is attitude, and attitude can make up for a lot of shortcomings. Just be sure to learn from your mistakes and don't repeat them. Ulysses S. Grant claimed, "I have acted in every instance from a conscientious desire to do what was right...and for the very best interests of the whole people. Failures have been errors of judgment, not of intent."[50] Robert W. Haack, leader of the New York Stock Exchange and later chairman of the Lockheed Corporation, cautioned that "the public may be willing to forgive us for mistakes in judgment but it will not forgive us for mistakes in motive."[51] Make sure yours are mistakes of mechanics, not character.

---

49 Geoff Colvin, "Why Talent Is Overrated," *Fortune*, October 21, 2008, http://archive.fortune.com/2008/10/21/magazines/fortune/talent_colvin.fortune/index.htm.

50 President Ulysses S. Grant's Farewell Address to Congress, 1876.

51 *The Wall Street Journal*, October 17, 1967.

The June 2006 issue of *The Atlantic Monthly* contains an article[52] by Matthew Stewart that's a worthwhile read. It questions the whole leadership consulting industry (amen). This is not the place to review it in detail, but Stewart basically argues that you don't have to get an MBA to be a leader—good common sense and some philosophy can take you a long way. Leadership, he says, is in large part about values, judgment, hard work, and personal commitment. There are no tricks, no secret sauce, no special inner sanctum where they'll take you when your time has come and initiate you into The Most Secret and Honorable Order of Leaders. Don't believe anyone who says he can teach you leadership in one hour, one course, or one book.

And it really helps if you can find a good mentor. Find a leader who demonstrates the attributes we've been discussing and just observe: How does she handle her staff? How does she make decisions? What are her values? Over and above passive observations, don't hesitate to seek her help. Good leaders will welcome the chance to lend a hand.

LEADERSHIP STYLE

There is no one-size-fits-all leader or leadership style. You don't necessarily have to be charismatic. You don't have to have the perfectly coiffed hair, the whitened teeth, or the thousand-dollar suits. Just show up with character, treat your troops right, and work hard. Most books on leadership enumerate traits (and this one is admittedly no different in that regard). Many researchers look for correlations between these traits, seeking the magic formula for the great leader. But these studies are almost always inconclusive, and that's really no great surprise. It's pretty simple, on the one hand, to see what you reap when you don't have the right character. But disappointing as it may be, there is no magic algorithm, no one set of traits or style that defines the successful leader. Rather than a magic algorithm or secret cure-all formula, the real secret

---

52 Matthew Stewart, "The Management Myth", *The Atlantic Monthly*, June 1, 2006.

is in learning to extract the right lessons from your reading of history, your experience, your observations. Then over time you can construct your own personal leadership style—the style that best integrates your personality, your experience, your situation, your environment.

Not all situations require the same style of leadership, and it's a fool's errand to try to remake yourself in the image of some cookie-cutter-manual leader. There is no universally good leader or style. Like it or not, you're stuck with yourself and where you are in life at this particular moment. Your task is best completed by looking ahead, drawing on past lessons, and not obsessing about genetic deficiencies or missed opportunities. The Roman philosopher Epictetus spoke of two kinds of things in life: those you can control and those you cannot. Your genes are your genes—your gender, your height, your native IQ, your eye color are not in your control. But arguably among those things *in* your control is the potential to make yourself into an effective leader or whatever else you put your mind to.

You've certainly heard the phrase *to command respect.* You command it in the sense that your actions *inspire* it rather than demanding that your troops respect you on the basis of position, rank, or *diktat* from higher authority. Remember: **A king does not command his men's loyalty through fear nor purchase it with gold; he earns their love by the sweat of his own back and the pains he endures for their sake.**

Writing on the influence of ancient philosophy—in particular the Stoics—on the military mind, Nancy Sherman draws on Cicero in regard to leadership style:

Just as differences in talent and temperament make specific career choices more or less appropriate, so too do individuals establish their distinctive styles and signatures...We might say that temperament puts pragmatic constraints on leadership style...Cicero suggests that diametrically opposed styles can be equally fitting expressions of excellence.... Cicero is keen to appeal to personality and temperament differences within civilian and military leadership roles as part of an implicit criticism of cookie-cutter views of what is fitting.

His roster of examples draws from the lives of public leaders: some, such as Socrates, are able to cultivate a sense of pretense and irony; others, including Pericles, the great Greek general of the Peloponnesian War, have authoritativeness without an ounce of levity. Certain leaders are distinguished for their cunning and craftiness...Others...are more "straightforward and open; they think that nothing should be done through secrecy or trickery, they cultivate the truth and they are hostile to deceit." And we should contrast Ulysses, who could suffer trial upon trial with patience and constancy, with Ajax, nicknamed the "bulwark of the Achaeans," who "would have preferred to seek death a thousand times than to endure such things." Some... "manage to appear in conversation to be one among many" despite their great power, while others of comparable stature are "not at all affable in conversation" and keep their distance from the minions. Cato, a paragon of austere self-discipline and constancy, seemed justified in committing suicide in the face of a tyrant, while others, "more gentle" and "easygoing" in their overall behavior, have less reason to do so even in the same...circumstances. Thus Cicero insists that the range of appropriate and permissible leadership styles is broad: "There are countless...dissimilarities of nature and conduct, which do not in the least deserve censure."[53]

So don't worry about fitting into some ideal leadership template. Create your own style—custom built, flexible, adaptable, but always anchored in the immutable principles of personal and professional integrity. Once you have crafted your leadership style—the core *you*—you

---

53 Nancy Sherman, *Stoic Warriors* (New York: Oxford University Press, 2005): 55.

can then adapt it to any given situation. Above all, *never give up*. That done, there are then about as many paths to becoming a leader as there are leaders.

LEADERSHIP CAPITAL

Regard your good name as the richest jewel you can possibly be possessed of, for credit is like fire; when once you have kindled it you may easily preserve it, but if you once extinguish it, you will find it an arduous task to rekindle it again. The way to gain a good reputation is to endeavor to be what you desire to appear.

Socrates

I referred earlier to the fact that you must not only possess these traits of a leader, you must be *seen* to have them. You will need a reputation for *ethos* (moral competence), so that what flies up from your anvil of truth will have weight. Repeated evidence of such ethos will result in your building up a store of "leadership capital" on which you can draw, like power out of a battery. You do this through an accretion of actions (and words) over time demonstrating your readiness to lead from the front, your care for your people, your willingness to fight for them. They must see that your professional skills are well developed and that you are always working to improve them. They must see that your judgment is good and that you put mission—and them—before self. While building up points in and of itself is not your object, you need to keep in mind that the troops will be closely observing your every move and consciously or unconsciously tallying up points on their mental balance sheets. No one is perfect, and not all your points will end up in the credit column—fair or not. But it's the net balance that counts over time. The more points you have in your leadership capital account, the more effectively you will be able to muster the leadership horsepower you need when the chips are down. And bear in mind what the seventeenth-century British author and philosopher Bishop Joseph Hall pointed out, "A reputation once broken may possibly be repaired, but the world will always keep their eyes on the spot where the crack was."

THE STRUGGLE TO BECOME A LEADER

It is not the critic who counts; not the man who points out how the strong man stumbles, or where the doer of deeds could have done them better. The credit belongs to the man who is actually in the arena, whose face is marred by dust and sweat and blood; who strives valiantly; who errs, who comes short again and again, because there is no effort without error and shortcoming; but who does actually strive to do the deeds; who knows great enthusiasms, the great devotions; who spends himself in a worthy cause; who at the best knows in the end the triumph of high achievement, and who at the worst, if he fails, at least fails while daring greatly, so that his place shall never be with those cold and timid souls who neither know victory nor defeat.

Theodore Roosevelt,
speech at the Sorbonne, Paris, April 23, 1910

From time immemorial, man has faced the same internal struggle between right and wrong, virtue and vice. Today is no different. You have no right to expect that it will be easy—quite the contrary, as is true of all the good things in life. Nothing worth having comes without hard work. This is what character is about—the voluntary act of choosing the right course of action, no matter the competing temptations. This struggle is no less relevant to leadership than other aspects of our existence.

Harking back to David Brooks's article on the philosopher's versus the psychologist's take on character, the distinction being drawn by some psychologists—that character is *situational*—is consistent with the relativism that has been eating away at the foundations of personal and national character in this country since the 1960s. This is nothing but a recycling of the old values battle. One side says there are moral absolutes, and we need to strive to achieve and maintain a character of integrity, elusive though this goal may prove. The other side says morals are situational and truth is relative. To me, the latter is nothing but a prescription for abandoning responsibility and accountability, inviting decadence and chaos. In this regard, I am not a philosopher, being deeply rooted in the day-to-day practical world where decisions must be taken—usually on short notice and without most of the relevant facts. But I am firmly in the camp of the philosophers in my belief that people's behavior is driven by values—or lack thereof—however tenuous our hold on them may be.

For the leader, the problem with the psychologist's view is that somewhere out there in the firmament, external to what the individual "feels," there exists this thing called the *real world* in which there is the right course of action and the wrong course of action, good and evil, the road to success and the road to failure. Actions and decisions affect real people and have serious, real-world consequences. If you act dishonorably, ducking responsibility or conspiring in your own self-interest, someone can end up getting badly hurt—person, community, country, or self. Where the leader comes down on this can spell the difference between success and failure.

Admittedly, there is no arguing with the psychologists' observation that we are all buffeted by internal passions, fears, and weaknesses. That said, society cannot afford for you as a leader to give yourself over to these demons, to kick back and disengage. That looks to me to be nothing more than burying your head in the sand, tuning out, and hoping reality will go away. That avoids the hard decisions we all must make. I'll leave it to the psychologists to offer excuses about how challenging it is to live a life of character these days—not that that's a novel insight—so long as they don't try to allow us to use it as an excuse to let ourselves off the hook. Moral relativism and postmodernism notwithstanding, decisions and actions have consequences, and the leader—and the people she leads—must live in that world.

Some of these psychologists contend that students who are routinely dishonest at home are not necessarily routinely dishonest at school. And they believe that people don't have one permanent thing called *character*, but rather have a "multiplicity of tendencies" inside, activated by this or that context. By accepting this situational ethic, a little bit of understanding can drag us quickly down the slippery slope, allowing us to rationalize overlooking a multitude of sins. Pretty soon, no one feels the need to act with integrity. If we could only ask the tens of millions who perished in World War II about the consequences of bad leadership and moral relativism…Would George Washington and our Founding Fathers have accepted this? Would Churchill? Would Martin Luther King, Jr.?

It is not that the person of character doesn't experience the instincts and impulses that have been "implanted by evolution culture, and upbringing."[54] Every one of us faces this, with whatever strength and backbone we can muster. It's not easy to command all the wild things duking it out inside our souls, but the real leader sucks it up and tries to do the right thing, even when it's not easy. By what right should you expect that life *should* be easy? Being a real leader means being in that morally difficult situation, recognizing in yourself those human weaknesses inherent in us all—the temptations that would induce us to take the easy road—and giving it your best to face them down. It means *not* behaving dishonorably. It means struggling to do the right thing for family, for the workforce, for country, for humanity, against whatever

---

54 Brooks, Where the Wild Things Are, *The New York Times.*

temptations or enemies you might face. You must take responsibility for your actions and not seek easy refuge behind the psychologists' skirts. It doesn't mean you're perfect—just that whatever the situation and whatever the fog of the moment, there is "honest" and "dishonest," distasteful as this concept might be to some critics. You might not always succeed, but at least you're giving it a shot, rather than finding false refuge in pop psychology. Blaming it all on the subconscious and whatever demons may in fact lie therein is nothing more than a cop-out. To give one's self over to these inner demons, weaknesses, fears, and dark passions is selfish, not selfless. There be dragons. Is that an example you want to set for your troops? I suspect you would instruct yours otherwise. And it is still not enough to achieve this mastery of yourself; you must demand it of others—above you, your peers, and below.

You have a choice when it comes to what kind of a leader you want to become.

Chapter 6

FROM THE TRIBE TO THE CLOUD: THE DIALECTIC OF COLLABORATION

I against my brother; I and my brother against my cousin; I and my brother and my cousin against the world.

Arab saying

In every field of endeavor, whatever the challenge, whatever the technology, the human factor reigns supreme. There are many dimensions, of course, to the human condition, but an element critically relevant to leadership is the collaborative—the ability to harness diverse talents, expertise, perspectives, and energies across multiple divisions, directorates, and agencies. Tribalism, on the other hand, is one of the most powerful, if primitive, aspects of human nature. It extends across organizations and works powerfully against collaboration. As a leader I have lost more stomach lining to tribal squabbles than to any other factor, including high-risk operations in denied areas. It is universal, ubiquitous, unpleasant, ugly, and just about any other *U* word you can come up with. It saps energy, stifles collaboration, and sabotages success. It exacerbates misunderstandings, elevates blood pressures, and eliminates opportunities. It gnaws away at the vital connective tissue that binds together the constituent parts of human enterprise. Did I mention that I think tribalism is a threat to organizational success? Here's Winston Churchill writing on the fiercely independent tribes of colonial India's North-West Frontier at the end of the nineteenth century:

> *The inhabitants of these wild...valleys are of many tribes, but of similar character and condition.... Except at the times of sowing and of harvest, a continual state of feud and strife prevails throughout the land. Tribe wars with tribe. The people of one valley fight with those of the next. To the quarrels of communities are added the combats of individuals. Khan assails khan, each supported by his retainers. Every tribesman has a blood feud with his neighbor. Every man's hand is against the other, and all against the stranger.*[55]

On the other hand, part of leadership involves instilling a sense of esprit de corps and specialness, a sense of elitism that can contribute greatly to your success. So the question is how to find the right balance between tribalism and collaboration—and harness the best of each.

---

55 Winston Churchill, *The Story of the Malakand Field Force* (London: Thomas Nelson & Sons, 1898).

This has been a critical time for the Intelligence Community—and, in fact, for all of government—in terms of forging real, working relationships between organizations. Tribalism is an issue that's always been with us. Whatever one thinks of the 9/11 Commission, the insularity and lack of collaboration in the Intelligence Community at the time was undeniable. Since then, on the positive side, the war on terrorism has given us some great examples of the tremendous power that can be unleashed through the orchestration of capabilities across the IC. But these examples notwithstanding, spirited struggles over turf continue to plague the Intelligence Community. I have come to realize that these same tribal frictions plague every organization on the face of the earth, numbering more than one person. As the Kingston Trio put it so tellingly in their song "The Merry Minuet":

The whole world is festering with unhappy souls.
The French hate the Germans, the Germans hate the Poles.
Italians hate Yugoslavs, South Africans hate the Dutch.
And I don't like anybody very much!

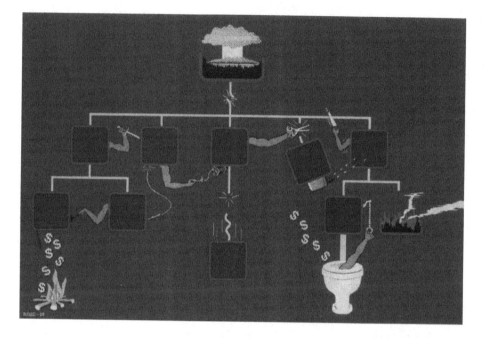

Figure 2. This is the "dysfunctional organization" chart I drew of a particularly fractious new political construct we were trying to shore up in a country with no functioning government some years ago. I subsequently deleted the organizational names, not for reasons of security, but because it perfectly reflects every organization I've ever worked with, in, or for.

Unarguably, the genetic adaptations favoring close-knit tribal groups were not without merit. Susan Okie is a physician, a former medical reporter, and the national science editor for the *Washington Post*. She is also a clinical assistant professor of family medicine at Georgetown University. In an article for the *Post* reviewing British evolutionary biologist Mark Pagel's *Wired for Culture: Origins of the Human Social Mind*, Okie discusses the transmission of culture within the tribe. Every word here is equally relevant to, and descriptive of, bureaucratic organizations, which have all the attributes of a tribe. She writes:

[O]ur remarkable longevity and reproductive success stem from our ability...to form close-knit tribal groups made up of

unrelated individuals who speak a common language.... Any newborn infant, born or adopted into any culture in the planet, will absorb the language, beliefs, values and norms of that society.... Pagel contends that we owe both our diverse talents as individuals and our success as a species to our ability to form cultures—tight social groups.... As Pagel writes, our cultures are "responsible for our art, music, and religion, our unmatched acts of chivalry...our sense of justice, fairness, altruism, and even self sacrifice"; but also for our self-interest, our ethnic and racial prejudices, our distrust of strangers, our wars.... [We]... cling tenaciously to loyalties and customs that differentiate us from our neighbors.... Through most of our history, our cultural groups have remained relatively small and cohesive, competing with other groups and typically fostering distrust of outsiders.[56]

Matt Ridley, who writes the *Wall Street Journal*'s weekly Mind and Matter column, also reviewed *Wired for Culture* and made similar observations on Pagel's thesis. As you read these words, think about your own organization:

Mark Pagel...sets out to explain this peculiar human property of fragmenting into mutually uncomprehending cultural groups.... The allegiance we feel to one tribe—religious, sporting, political, linguistic, even racial—is a peculiar mixture of altruism toward the group and hostility to other groups. Throughout history, united groups have stood, while divided ones fell.[57]

These perspectives sound pretty much on the mark to me. Think of the military, fraternities and sororities, and social clubs: they all

---

56 Susan Okie, review of *Wired for Culture: Origins of the Human Social Mind*, by Mark Pagel, *Washington Post*, January 23, 2012, http://www.washingtonpost.com/politics/.

57 Matt Ridley, "Why Our Culture Is in Our Genes," *Wall Street Journal*, March 2, 2012, http://www.wsj.com/articles/SB10001424052970204653604577249464154315128.

go to varying lengths to strip away your previous identity and forge in you a new one that aligns with the group. These groups have their own jargon, rituals, oaths, codes, ways of dressing, and ways (often secret) of identifying each other—all measures to encourage you to bond strongly with the group. From the day of induction, all elite organizations work to foster, encourage, and inculcate a sense of specialness, of pride, of looking out for each other which, in turn, promotes courage, dedication, and selflessness. The credo of the US Coast Guard reads, in part:

I am proud to be a United States Coast Guardsman.

I revere that long line of expert seamen who by their devotion to duty and sacrifice of self have made it possible for me to be a member of a service honored and respected, in peace and in war, throughout the world.

I never, by word or deed, will bring reproach upon the fair name of my service, nor permit others to do so unchallenged.

This is the kind of spirit that the leader wants to instill in those she leads. Inevitably…necessarily, this involves the concept of "the other," real or imagined. These others—other fraternities, other universities, other teams, other ethnic groups—serve as a target on which the "tribe" can focus its hostility, thereby reinforcing the obligation for tribal cohesion. Authoritarian regimes have perfected the myth of external interference in their internal affairs—"the foreign hand"—to divert the attention of their suffering masses from their own political and economic shortcomings. Much time and energy is spent extolling the virtues of the group and demonizing the opposition. To a certain degree, loyalty and bonding within the group are directly proportional to the hostility toward "the other"—the more you demonize the other, the more you need the safety, solidarity, and comfort of the group.

This universal distrust of the "them" is not unique to our era. What Pagel describes is, I believe, hardwired into our DNA, going back a hundred thousand years. When you saw that guy from another tribe coming over the hill, it was imperative to get your spear in his gut first because the only reason he was coming over the hill was to put his spear in *your* gut, steal your cattle, and carry off your women. People learned to band together in close kinship groups, clans, and tribes for security and to instinctively distrust the outsider. Those who followed this dictum survived; those who greeted the intruder with open arms were summarily removed from the gene pool.

It should be in no way surprising, then, to see these same pervasive and deeply rooted tribal factors fueling contemporary bureaucratic warfare. And—wherever you are, caught in perpetual conflict between organizations—don't for a minute think it is unique to your situation. It's equally rampant in academia, industry, medicine, and every other aspect of society. These tribal instincts are one of the most primal factors in the human condition, present in all social groupings, at all times, in all societies. And, regrettably, it will always be thus. During the Cold War, I recall reading about the enmity between KGB (the civilian intelligence service in the old Soviet Union) and Soviet Military Intelligence—the GRU. According to a popular BBC series on television, British MI5 and MI6 detest each other (when they're not ganging up on the British Signals Intelligence organization GCHQ and, of course, the CIA). And, if there are extraterrestrials preparing an imminent invasion of Earth, I'm sure they're up there right now bickering over who gets to launch the first photon torpedo and who will get dominion over New Jersey.

I recently came across a fascinating article in the *Weekly Standard*, a review of a book called *Culture and Conflict in the Middle East*, by Philip Carl Salzman. This thoughtful, fourteen-page review, written by Stanley Kurtz, gives an account of the role tribalism plays in Arab and other tribal cultures (including the Pushtun tribes of the Pakistan-Afghanistan border area), which in and of itself is riveting. But over and above the insights into tribalism in South Asia, reading this article you will note that the bureaucratic warfare we find throughout today's society is remarkably similar to the tribal dynamics Kurtz describes...and seems equally unlikely to disappear. Kinsmen will band together to take up the defense of an offended kinsman and aggressively confront (with threat of violence) "the other." When a dispute arises with someone from another tribal entity, all kinsmen will bond together to protect the group—only to fall back into internal disharmony once "they" are dealt with and out of the picture. Each member of the group is honor bound to side with other members of the immediate kinship group against the more distant group.[58] So it goes in our society today: members of one organization standing firmly against "the other," that is until "the other" is removed, at which point they happily return to scratching each other's eyes out in-house (only a slight hyperbole).

Before he retired, my father, a cardiologist, was appointed chief of medicine at a major hospital in our hometown. A short time later, the state mandated that two hospitals, including my father's, merge into one. My father dutifully set about working to organize his colleagues to this end...with zero success. After several agonizing years of squabbling, during which some doctors from hospital *A* wouldn't even talk to doctors from hospital *B*, everyone finally gave up, and the state ended up having to build yet another hospital. Recalling my father's tales of dysfunction, I would later tell him that I only had to change the names of the organizations to describe what I saw happening in the government. Accounts by my sister, a professor of composition at a major university, of the battles between the composition and English literature factions within her department were even worse. I gave my father and sister framed copies of my dysfunctional organization chart (see above).

So the logical question will be: How does this affect you as a leader? How does tribalism relate to collaboration and leadership, and what do you do about it? Well, another recent Matt Ridley article, this one in the

---

58 Stanley Kurtz, "I and My Brother against My Cousin," review of *Culture and Conflict in the Middle East*, by Philip Carl Salzman, *Weekly Standard*, April 14, 2008, http://www.weeklystandard.com/Content/Public/Articles/000/000/014/947kigpp.asp.

Wall Street Journal, describes the collaborative yang to the yin of tribalism. The article, "From Phoenicia to Hayek to the 'Cloud,'" was adapted from Ridley's Hayek Prize lecture, given under the auspices of the Manhattan Institute in September 2011. Ridley writes of what he calls

> *the crowd-sourced, wikinomic cloud...Human technological advancement depends not on individual intelligence but on collective idea sharing.... Human progress waxes and wanes according to how much people connect and exchange.... Knowledge is dispersed and shared. Friedrich Hayek was the first to point out, in his famous 1945 essay "The Use of Knowledge in Society," that central planning cannot work because it is trying to substitute an individual all-knowing intelligence for a distributed and fragmented system of localized but connected knowledge.... So dispersed is knowledge that, as Leonard Read famously observed in his 1958 essay "I, Pencil," nobody on the planet knows how to make a pencil. The knowledge is dispersed among many thousands of graphite miners, lumberjacks, assembly line workers, ferrule designers, salesmen, and so on. This is true of everything I use in my everyday life, from my laptop to my shirt to my city. Nobody knows how to make it or to run it. Only the cloud knows.... One of the things I have tried to do is...take this insight as far back into the past as I can—to try to understand when it first began to be true. When did human beings start to use collective rather than individual intelligence? In doing so, I find the entire field of anthropology and archeology needs Hayek badly. Their debates about what made human beings successful, and what caused the explosive take-off of human culture in the past 100,000 years, simply never include the insight of dispersed knowledge.... They are still looking inside human heads rather than between them.... There was a sudden change in brain size 200,000 years ago. We Africans—all human beings are descended chiefly from people who lived exclusively in Africa until about 65,000 years ago—had slightly smaller brains than the*

Neanderthals, yet once outside Africa we rapidly displaced them... and the reason we won the war against the Neanderthals, if war it was, is staring us in the face...we exchanged. It gave us the edge over Neanderthals in their own continent and their own climate, because good ideas can spread through trade.... You are drawing upon ideas that occurred to anybody anywhere anytime within your...network. Trade...creates a collective innovating brain as big as the trade network itself. When you cut people off from exchange networks, their innovation rate collapses.[59]

For civilization to advance required the imposition of some sort of order (not always commensurate with justice). As Steven Pinker, author of popular best sellers including *The Blank Slate* and *How the Mind Works*, writes in the *Wall Street Journal*, "it's not that the first kings had a benevolent interest in the welfare of their citizens. Just as a farmer tries to keep his livestock from killing one another, so a ruler will try to keep his subjects from cycles of raiding and feuding. From his point of view, such squabbling is a dead loss—foregone opportunities to extract taxes, tribute, soldiers and slaves." Not without some trepidation, I am inclined to disagree with the main thrust of Pinker's argument—that "we may be living in the most peaceable era in human history...[B]rutality is declining and empathy is on the rise."

The forces for order have made great, though greatly uneven, strides over the millennia in tamping down the pernicious forces of tribalism, racism, and other forms of discrimination, but I would suggest that for the most part this has been the application, by parents and social institutions, of merely the thinnest veneer of civilization, with the weakest of adhesive, subject to being ripped away at the least perturbation. Pinker rightly points to a "cascade of 'rights revolutions'—a growing revulsion

---

59 Matt Ridley, "From Phoenicia to Hayek to the 'Cloud,'" *Wall Street Journal*, September 24–25, 2011, http://www.wsj.com/articles/SB10001424053111903703604576588500559039210.

against aggression on smaller scales. In the developed world, the civil rights movement obliterated lynchings and lethal pogroms."[60]

Perhaps, but don't think for a moment that the Dark Side of the Force has ceded the field. For evidence, look at the research into mob rule, how our inhibitions dissolve in the crowd. Look at the Holocaust. Look at the bloody massacres in the wake of Indian independence in 1947. Look at the ethnic cleansing and genocide in the Balkans and Rwanda in the mid-1990s. Look at the recent barbarous religious and ethnic cleansing by the so-called Islamic State in Syria and Iraq. Who would have thought that, in the twenty-first century, one "tribe" would be gunning down, beheading, even crucifying women and children for refusing to submit to its perverted idea of religion? As for the "developed world"—on a less lethal scale, though still demonstrative—look what happens when one team loses a national championship, and the crowds leave the sports bars to loot and burn. In the massive devastation and flooding that followed Hurricane Katrina in New Orleans in 2005, we witnessed an incredible display of charity and people helping their neighbors. On the other hand,

New Orleans Mayor Ray Nagin ordered 1,500 police officers to leave their search-and-rescue mission Wednesday night and return to the streets of the beleaguered city to stop looting that has turned increasingly hostile.

"They are starting to get closer to heavily populated areas—hotels, hospitals and we're going to stop it right now," Nagin said in a statement to The Associated Press.

Looters used garbage cans and inflatable mattresses to float away with food, blue jeans, tennis shoes, TV sets—even guns. Outside

---

60 Steven Pinker, "Violence Vanquished," *Wall Street Journal*, September 24, 2011, http://www.wsj.com/articles/SB10001424053111904106704576583203589408180.

one pharmacy, thieves commandeered a forklift and used it to push up the storm shutters and break through the glass. The driver of a nursing-home bus surrendered the vehicle to thugs after being threatened.

Police were asking residents to give up any firearms before they evacuated neighborhoods because officers desperately needed the firepower: Some officers who had been stranded on the roof of a hotel said they were shot at.

Police said their first priority remained saving lives, and mostly just stood by and watched the looting. But Nagin later said the looting had gotten so bad that stopping the thieves became the top priority for the police department.[61]

William Golding's classic novel *Lord of the Flies* was an examination of what happens when a group of British boys are left to their own devices on an island. They devolve into a band of brutal, sadistic savages. Progress toward peace and collaboration in modern times is no mean accomplishment, but these accomplishments should not be overestimated or taken for granted, and the ever-present threat of tribalism is left unaddressed at our collective peril.

So there is something of a dialectic here that the leader must reconcile—tribal forces in a very real sense have served us quite well historically. They help us build good communities and contribute to esprit de corps. Tribalism, still today, offers the security needed to survive in primitive societies in which there is no social order or system of justice—where might rules. And certainly there are forces today that are reinforcing and magnifying tribal fractionalization: that universal connector, the Internet, allows us to hook up with those like us on Facebook

---

61 Associated Press, "New Orleans Mayor Orders Looting Crackdown," NBCNews.com, September 9, 2005, http://www.nbcnews.com/id/9063708/.

and web pages that focus on our specific interests and ever-more-narrowly focused social groups. Cable TV news and discussion programs cater to ever-narrower demographics and interest groups vice broad audiences. On the other hand, cloud collaboration offers tremendous advantages to mission accomplishment. Extraordinarily complex problems that have defied our best scientists' attempts to solve them can now be put out on the Internet (so-called crowdsourcing—where hundreds, if not thousands, of people can contribute to the solution), with marked success.

The analogy to the workplace is obvious. Individual elements, components, programs, and agencies can only profit from "intertribal trade"—trade in ideas, methodology, data, and personnel—harnessing the "cloud." To remain insular is to die out. To paraphrase Ridley's conclusion, human collaboration is necessary for your organization to work; authoritarian, insular tribal rule is the enemy of order, progress, and success in your particular field and in society at large.

This dialectic between tribal security and elitism on the one hand and altruistic, collaborative outreach on the other is nicely laid out in Paul J. Zak's book *The Moral Molecule*, in which he makes the case that there is a chemical basis for collaboration that evolved to foster prosperity, tribal instincts to the contrary notwithstanding. The chemical is oxytocin, and Zak argues that it evolved for the purpose of strengthening social bonds in mammals. In reviewing Zak's book, Michael Shermer in the *Wall Street Journal* describes how

countries whose citizens trust one another gain economically, enjoying a higher gross domestic product, on average, than countries where lower levels of trust exist.... Zak explains that trust is built through mutually beneficial exchanges that result in higher levels of oxytocin...Zak identifies a causal chain from oxytocin to empathy to morality to trust to economic flourishing.... Experiments that Mr. Zak has conducted in his lab...show that subjects who are cooperative and generous in a trust game begin the activity with higher levels of oxytocin than other participants. And infusing the latter with oxytocin through a nose spray causes their generosity and cooperativeness to increase.[62]

(Immediately on reading this article, I ordered twenty-five cases of said nasal spray for my Program. Coming soon to a pharmacy near you.)

When Zak took blood samples before and after a wedding to investigate changes in oxytocin, he found significantly elevated levels in the bride and parents. Interestingly, the level of oxytocin in the groom rose only 19 percent; this is because the male hormone testosterone interferes with oxytocin, which would go a long way to explain a lot of male posturing, pugnacity, and other tribal behaviors—from the jungles of New Guinea to the corridors of power in Washington, DC.

Finally, don't allow yourself to get disheartened. As I noted above, if you're going to tackle the tough jobs, it is important to remember that bureaucratic dissention does not plague your organization alone; it is a universal fact of life. It seems to be these days that my chief function in my Program is less to manage operations than to fight the strong, centrifugal tribal forces that constantly threaten to send parts of the Program flying off into the void. But *understanding that tribalism is ubiquitous is no excuse for giving ourselves over to it.* As a leader, unless you can somehow master tribalism across organizations *and* in yourself, your undertaking is doomed to mediocrity. Fighting our primeval tribal instincts is a full-time job, and it will take...*leadership*—consistent, persistent, and insistent—from the very top of the organization down. And don't feel guilty if you yourself experience these feelings; you're only human. It's no sin to *have* these feelings; it's only a sin to give in to them. Be always on the alert for these inclinations in yourself and in your troops, and work to rise above them. This will take conscious attention, mission focus, and discipline, along with consummate political

---

62 Michael Shermer, "Kin and Kindness," review of *The Moral Molecule*, by Paul J. Zak, *Wall Street Journal*, May 25, 2012, http://www.wsj.com/articles/SB10001424052702304723304577 367920639482882.

skill, won through years of bruising, disheartening bureaucratic combat, along with a few spears in the gut and knives in the back. But persevere. If everyone gives in to the admittedly natural instincts of tribalism, no organization can succeed, and society will suffer.

There is no question of conquering tribalism; the best you can hope for is to recognize it, shine the harsh spotlight of your leadership on it, and work proactively every day to keep it in a hammerlock. When it manages to wriggle free, as it inevitably will, saddle up your posse and wrangle it quickly back into custody until it again escapes to do its evil work. Never let your guard down. If you can't rise above it, your undertaking will be an engine working at 10 percent efficiency, with 90 percent of your energy ground up in internal friction.

My point? Tribalism is here to stay, at least until evolution works it out of the gene pool in about seventy-five thousand years. Like everything else, it has its good side and bad. Collaboration has a similar basis in evolution. The two forces are entwined in our DNA. The job for the leader is to manage these forces and lead the troops to maximum performance by harnessing the best of each force and mitigating the worst. Man is capable of moderating tribalistic instincts, although like an electromagnetic field, the leader's influence falls off with the square of the distance, and it takes considerable energy to maintain the field and keep the "particles" (troops) in alignment. Any weakening of the field will result in the particles going random again, with resultant organizational chaos (and failure).

Collaboration—Ridley's "cloud"—can vastly improve the effectiveness of our efforts and our lives. Crank up your collaborative field generator, encourage others to alter their attitudes, and leverage collaboration to achieve success. Just as West Point and the Naval Academy do, exchange hostages, live the other guy's existence and learn, meet face-to-face (video conferencing only goes so far; you need human contact to overcome the tribal DNA). Remember in those late-evening bull sessions that, contrary to what you all accuse them of, the other guys are most likely loyal Americans, probably as smart as you, equally dedicated, and certainly equally as convinced that their way is the best; and in their late-night bull session across town, they're having the same conversation about how frustrated they are with those shortsighted bureaucrats on the other side (you) who just can't see things the right (i.e., their) way. To an astonishing degree, this is an exercise in enlightenment and attitude. It doesn't take fancy courses, machines, consultants, legions of "human resources" (ugh…what ever happened to the perfectly well-named personnel department?), facilitators, or money. A leader must learn to achieve this balance of collaboration and tribal esprit de corps.

There are clear examples in my world of intelligence collection that illustrate beyond doubt the immense power and force-multiplier effect of well-thought-out and well-led collaboration. I have seen it handled poorly, and I have seen it handled well, and it's astonishing what can be achieved when it's the latter. You will find it a subtle, nuanced balance—not a black and white—thing. Most of all, it's about attitude: "those bastards across the river" as opposed to "members of my team in the shield wall, facing the common foe."

Chapter 7

CONCLUSION–LEADERSHIP THROUGH INTEGRITY

My Marine service was a life-changing experience for me. A positive one that had I not had, I most likely would not be standing here today...In that diverse company I learned to be responsible for others, I learned to depend on others, and to understand what being depended on by others really meant. I learned that there was more to the world than me, and my kind...I learned there was joy and satisfaction to be had by looking past the mirror. By serving common interests rather than only those of self...[m]y three years of service connected me to the rest of the world, the world outside myself, and the connection has been permanent.

Jim Lehrer, former Marine,

Harvard commencement speech, June 8, 2006

At this point, it's reasonable for you to ask: Why should I accept this concept of leadership through integrity? While I believe integrity has an intrinsic value outside the realm of leadership, that ethical debate is for another time and place. After all, you are not being paid simply to be a leader or for your sterling character, but to apply that leadership and character to produce results. The relevant question, then, is this: Can a "pragmatic" case be demonstrated that you will be more effective in producing these results if you lead with integrity as opposed to a "values-neutral" course?

Assuming an adequate measure of the other requisite traits, I have contended that you will, in fact, be a considerably more effective leader if you establish yourself as a person of character. If people have taken your measure and judged you to be a person of integrity, you will have a sufficient store of leadership capital to command the troops. For all the reasons laid out above, well-led troops will be more effective. People will argue that leaders of a lesser character can still be great, so let's turn that around and consider the question from the reverse angle: Can you imagine an organization as being successful and effective if led by an untrustworthy, self-serving narcissist? If it's hard to be a good leader and succeed against the odds, it's surprisingly easy for a bad leader to destroy an organization. A reputation for integrity will motivate your team to follow you into harm's way. A reputation for integrity will help you build up allies (people who trust you, whom you have helped and who will, in turn, be willing to help you in time of need). A reputation for integrity will help you carry the day when you are pitching your chain of command to adopt some bold course of action in the face of institutional obstructionism.

Having gone to some length to stake out this position, I felt an obligation to try to substantiate it in some objective sense, more than just inferring it from several decades of serving under good and bad leaders and occupying various positions of leadership myself. It would be most convenient if this argument lent itself to a nice, formal, objective, logical proof. Regrettably, it does not, at least not one that I could apprehend.

In lieu of such a formal approach, I'll return to probably the greatest leader in the history of our country—George Washington, a paragon of character, virtue, and selflessness if there ever was one. In the *American Daily Advertiser* on September 19, 1796, Washington wrote a farewell letter to the American people. It read, in part:

> *Of all the dispositions and habits which lead to* political prosperity, *religion and morality are indispensable supports. In vain would that man claim the tribute of patriotism, who should labor to subvert these great pillars of human happiness, the firmest props of the duties of men and citizens...It is substantially true that virtue or morality is a necessary spring of popular government. The rule, indeed, extends with more or less force to* every *species of free* government.[63] *[Emphasis mine.]*

If I may presume to extrapolate from Washington here, I think it not unfair to substitute *good leadership* for *political prosperity* and later for *free government* without doing a disservice to his intent. At the risk of coming across as naive and Pollyannaish, I would argue that if we strive to make integrity the foundation of all human interaction, that's as much a guarantor of success as is possible in this uncertain life. Religion aside, it is difficult to imagine an effective and successful moral framework for society based on individual moral relativism and "non-judgmentalism." Leadership against the toughest challenges requires, as C. S. Lewis argued, a "shared" moral framework—of which integrity is the mortar that holds the bricks together, something that must be passed down through some social institution—taught, honored, and defended. We allow this mortar to crumble from our foundation at our peril and, regrettably, societal forces in the country today seem to be leading us in this wrong direction.

---

63 George Washington's Farewell Address, 1796, http://avalon.law.yale.edu/18th_century/washing.asp.

At its heart, real leadership (and real "followership," for that matter) is about duty and obligation, not prestige, honors, or compensation. You shouldn't think about it in terms of titles, perquisites, prestige, or money. Duty is not about your gratification and enjoyment. Duty can be intimidating, at times painful. Duty is about what you must do because it is the right thing to do for the greater good, regardless of the implications for you. You may not end up with acclaim, credit, or reward, but motivation for real leaders comes from the heart, not the thirst for power, fame, or riches.

What's relevant to the aspiring young leader is not the libraries full of books on leadership, the lists, the ten-step methods, the thirty-day course to leadership. For millennia, scholars have studied leadership, looking for secrets, innate attributes, formulae, and correlations of character traits to effectiveness. So what should *you* do? There is no simple set of rules, no universal checklist you can mold yourself to. You must take your principles, your personality, your history, and your genes and construct your own style as a leader. Yes, different personalities and styles will be better or worse, and, in fact, in different situations different leaders with different personalities and different styles will be better than in other situations. But you can't be someone you are not; you can only be who you are. That said, there is no reason that, given the right values, some intelligence, open ears, an empathetic heart, and a great deal of hard work, you can't become an effective, respected leader in the true sense of the word. Circumstances, missions, colleagues, and bosses may change, but you can learn to develop your core leadership values and fashion your style. Hold to that core, hold to those universals discussed in this book, maintain your integrity—these are your constants in a changing world.

When you find yourself facing one of those challenges, those intractable problems, think about these great leaders. Read biographies of people like Churchill, General George Marshall, Steve Jobs, and other great leaders throughout history, and take their lesson. No, they were not perfect; nor will you be. But there is a common thread, an attitude, an approach to life that they shared. Don't shrink from tough missions. Learn how to deconstruct the hard problems and solve them in detail. Summon the energy to take the hard road (a road most definitely less traveled.) Create that vision; mobilize and motivate your troops. Earn the confidence and respect of your troops. Look after them and put their welfare ahead of yours. Live and lead by the rules of the Spartans at Thermopylae.

Steven Hayward, of the American Enterprise Institute, has written a book about what it takes to make a great leader, building on the lives and careers of Winston Churchill and Ronald Reagan. In it he talks about character:

Greatness is ultimately a question of character. Good character does not change with the times: it has eternal qualities...The tides of history and the scale of modern life have not made obsolete or incommensurate the kind of large-souled greatness we associate with Churchill or Lincoln or George Washington...Why were Churchill and Reagan virtually alone among their contemporaries in their particular insights and resolves? The answer must be that they transcended their environments and transformed their circumstances as only great men can do, and thereby bent history to their will...

And so we have our answer to the question often voiced today: Can there be another Churchill, or another Reagan? The answer is plainly yes...[Their] example of the possibility of human greatness is not bound by time or circumstance.[64]

It is extraordinarily difficult to lead at the top level. It's not just the mission that is difficult, but the human elements, politics, and tribalism

---

64 Steven F. Hayward, *Greatness: Reagan, Churchill, and the Making of Extraordinary Leaders* (New York: Crown Forum, 2005).

that introduce major impediments. The external problem itself often pales in comparison with the internal difficulties managing your team. But that's exactly what leadership is about, and it's why we need leaders of the ilk described in this book. In the end, it's up to you to choose what kind of leader you will be. Be strong, be persistent, never give up. Take care of your people. Be methodical and creative, not only in *solving* the problem, but in *defining* it. Think of what can *be* rather than what *is*. Don't just accept what everyone else believes—think it out for yourself. And by no means accept the conventional wisdom of what is possible and what is not. In all this, integrity acts as a force multiplier; on the other hand, lack of integrity acts as a retardant, friction, sand in the gears. Character counts, and character will earn you the consent of the led.

A vital part of becoming a leader is developing the ability to stand up to what Edwin Friedman, a Jewish rabbi and family therapist, characterizes as "resistance." Far from my being the Lone Ranger on the resistance frontier, I learned that Friedman's research identifies as widespread the same foot-dragging and risk aversion I have encountered in my career. Friedman points out that he identified the same (usually ineffective) approaches to leadership virtually everywhere his research took him (religious communities, state government, business, and military). He strongly counseled against the highly anxious risk avoider, more adept at dodging conflict than the nimblest running back:

> *The more my perspective broadened, the more confirmed I became in my view that contemporary leadership dilemmas have less to do with the specificity of given problems, the nature of a particular technique, or the makeup of a given group than with the way everyone is framing the issues...*

> *In any type of institution whatsoever, when a self-directed, imaginative, energetic, or creative member is being consistently frustrated and sabotaged rather than encouraged and supported,*

what will turn out to be true one hundred percent of the time, regardless of whether the disrupters are supervisors, subordinates, or peers, is that the person at the very top of that institution is a peace-monger. By that I mean a highly anxious risk-avoider, someone who is more concerned with good feelings than with progress, someone whose life revolves around the axis of consensus, a "middler,"... someone who treats conflict or anxiety like mustard gas—one whiff, on goes the emotional gas mask, and he flits.
This principle of organizational life is so universal it may be rooted in protoplasm itself.[65]

Friedman goes on to cite five important characteristics of an effective leader:

- The persistence to face inertial resistance

- The capacity to obtain clarity about one's principles and vision

- The capacity to separate oneself from surrounding emotional processes

- The willingness to be exposed and be vulnerable

- The self-regulation of emotions in the face of reactive sabotage

As detailed in an earlier chapter, the real leader must steel herself to have the courage of her convictions, to grapple with conflict actively, vice wearing herself out in shuttle diplomacy attempting to achieve "compromise." Peace in our time didn't work all that well at Munich; it won't work in your organization. Real leaders have to lead, to be strong. Real leaders don't put a finger up to test the wind. Real leaders show people the path toward mission accomplishment. Real leaders don't consult the polls or adapt to the majority "solution." It never really does turn out to be a solution.

---

65 Edwin H. Friedman, *A Failure of Nerve* (New York: Seabury, 2007).

Being tough and strong is easy enough when you're winning. But it's another thing entirely when you're facing adversity, when you have to pick yourself up—however disheartened, however dispirited—and rejoin the fight. Leadership is often about doing things you'd really rather not do. This is true from your personal perspective, but even more important for those you lead.

As leaders—as humans—we are every bit as susceptible as those we lead to demoralization and discouragement, but you must make every effort to control it not only inwardly, but to control any outward manifestation of these sentiments. After all, if they see you give up, why would they press on? We have introduced this thinking into the training for our Program. Part of it involves a week on a simulated operation, out in bad weather, with little sleep, and in the face of intense pressure and confusion. Our teams face mental and physical challenges designed to take them well out of their comfort zones. One of these involves events on a high ropes course, bringing out in many a natural apprehension about heights. In our prebrief, we explain that the ropes course was built by one of the best construction companies in the business with an unblemished reputation for safety. Our training cadre, most of them ex-military special-operations combat veterans, are highly trained in these kinds of evolutions, and the course and individual equipment are inspected carefully before every use. That eliminates all real factors generating stress in the students, leaving only what's between their ears. It becomes a battle between their fear and their commitment to mission accomplishment—a good metaphor for real-world operations.

In the commercial ropes course world, they have a principle called Challenge by Choice. This means that if you get forty feet up on the apparatus and they ask you to take a leap out into the void, you can elect to back down, and they will "support" you. We explain that that's not at all how our training works. Why, we ask, would we spend the taxpayers' money on building the ropes course, take our valuable team members out on the course, put them in stressful situations, and then accept that they should leave at the end of the day having backed down and failed?

Our approach is to put them in that situation, where they would rather be any place other than on the precipice, where they'd really like to quietly back down, and then help them successfully see it through. Then we want them to take that experience back to the office and summon up that same determination when they face a similarly stressful challenge in an operation. This is because they will regularly encounter situations in our work where they really, really would rather not face the unpleasantness or risk. But in our business—and in yours—that doesn't get the job done. Your "operations" can't succeed unless your teams are undeterred by risk and danger (and not just in the physical sense, it applies to any leader and team that take on hard challenges).

Our training cadre has an almost-perfect record in getting people through these stressful evolutions. We've had people whose whole career had been spent in front of a computer, who had never even heard the word "rappelling," who left the course not only having rappelled, but rappelled Australian style—that is, standing on the very edge of the cliff, facing outward, feeding rope out until (still at the top of the cliff) their bodies are parallel to the ground with their faces downward, and then feeding the rope through a belay device to lower themselves to the ground. (Sorry, it's almost as hard to describe as it is to do in fact.)[66] In other challenges in the course, people who had never put their faces in the water accomplished missions swimming through barriers underwater in total darkness. A very high percentage of our students say this was the best training they had ever undergone in their careers, and we get constant feedback from alumni to the effect that they are much more confident in facing work challenges after the course. It clearly accomplishes our goal of preparing our officers to never give up on a mission.

This lesson is by no means limited to the kind of work we do in our Program. Facing one's fears having the courage of one's convictions are attributes that are critical for taking on life's many challenges and going

---

66 For a demonstration, check out this YouTube video: http://www.youtube.com/watch?v=yp38DGBH134.

on with life in the face of defeat, loss, and opposition—at work or at home. This is the job of a leader—to train her people to face tough situations and then, whatever the setback or adversity, to set the example of courage and grace under pressure, to never give up. Particularly as a leader, you have to discipline yourself in terms of what attitudes you project: no matter how discouraged or disheartened you may be, you must do your best to maintain a positive demeanor. We all have experienced this fear—I certainly have. We're discouraged; we feel like quitting. If you're not the leader, you may get away with indulging these sentiments and wallowing in self-pity. But if you're the leader, you have no such luxury. Dispiritedness, despair, discouragement—it's the most contagious of diseases, and most often fatal to the mission.

In May 1949, Dr. Douglas Southall Freeman (1886–1953), a newspaper editor and Civil War scholar noted for writing a Pulitzer Prize–winning four-volume biography of Robert E. Lee, gave a powerful lecture at the Naval War College in Newport, Rhode Island on leadership. The speech is every bit as applicable today as it was sixty-four years ago. Freeman had an instinctive skepticism of formal psychology regarding leadership, seeing things in much simpler, more practical terms. Beginning his lecture speaking of George Washington, Freeman said:

He exemplified leadership, which is not anything like as complicated as some of the psychologists would make it out to be…Leadership is fundamentally common sense…it consists fundamentally of three things and three only. If a man meets these three conditions, he is going to be a leader; if he fails to meet them, he may be on the roster as the head of a command, but he will never be at the head of the command when it marches down the pages of history—never!

First, know your stuff…know your specialty, know your…history. Number two…be a man…and that means a man of character…a man of industry…a man of fair play. Last of all, the third point. Look after your men.

Have I oversimplified this case? I think sometimes we overcomplicate it. I think sometimes we take these books on psychology, we take all the arts of salesmanship and we try to apply them...in a manner that is too elaborate...Look after your men. What a simple thing you are saying![67]

In this book, I have made the case for integrity in life and leadership, the kind of integrity shown by the greatest leaders in our history—from Washington to Lincoln to Churchill to countless great men and women whose names and accomplishments will never be broadly known or recognized. But these last are no less leaders of character. You have met them at home, at school, at work. Be they figures on the national stage or simply your brother or sister, integrity stands at the core of service to family, nation, and mankind. You know them; you know the good leaders, you know the bad. As Freeman pointed out, it's not rocket science: duty, honor, country, courage, commitment. Value family, value honor, and value dedication to doing the right thing. Choose the way of integrity.

* * *

The following quote was found in the field notebook of a young Marine 1st Lieutenant killed in action near Fallujah, Iraq, in September 2004.

I hope that my achievements in life shall be these—that I will have fought for what was right and fair, that I will have risked for that which mattered, that I will have given help to those who were in need, and that I will have left the earth a better place for what I've done and who I've been.

C. Hoppe

I can think of no higher standard to strive for, and character and integrity will take you a long way on that journey. Godspeed, leader.

---

67 Douglas Southall Freeman, "Leadership," a lecture delivered at the Naval War College, May 11, 1949, published in *Naval War College Review* 32 (April 1979).

ACKNOWLEDGMENTS

A book is rarely the product of one person, and this one is no different. Throughout my life, more people than can be named here inspired me, encouraged me, showed me the way. They were friends, relatives, bosses, coworkers, and role models. Writing this book was a matter of putting down on paper what they taught me by personal example, a debt far beyond my ability to repay.

First, Doris, my wife and loving companion through almost half a century of adventures at home and around the world, and a leader in her own right. One of the great secrets of our business, one that I will readily disclose, is that our spouses play an enormously important role in our lives and work overseas. This was certainly true in my case, on many a back street on many a dark night. Add to that bouts of dengue fever and dysentery, with occasional retreats to the safe haven in the face of anti-American riots. And this says nothing of trying to raise a family with some semblance of normality in those precincts. Whatever I may have achieved, it would never have happened had we not met.

My parents, to whom I owe everything that I may have become and accomplished, superb leaders themselves. My sisters, Mary and Louise, an author and professor of composition and a patient counselor in my Odyssean quest for publication. Adorable Hal, Sydney, and Alexandra—future leaders who remind me every day why life is worth living.

Throughout my career I have had the great fortune to serve under men and women who set me on the right course and showed—by example, not words—what true leadership really is. These anonymous heroes, whose contributions to the nation are as significant as they are unsung, have served as examples for generations of intelligence professionals. There are far too many to include here, to say nothing of the fact that most cannot be named, but they include George Tenet, former Director of Central Intelligence, whose steadfastness and courage gave us top cover when the going got tough and who, when many around him were looking to the exits, never lost faith in us; Admiral William O. Studeman, USN, Ret., former Deputy Director of Central Intelligence, a visionary thinker, ahead of his time, whose leadership gave me and many others the opportunity for the career of a lifetime—without his encouragement and support, this book would have never seen the light of day; LtGen John F. Sattler, USMC, Ret.—a true warrior, recognized as one of the most esteemed leaders in the Marine Corps, who provided encouragement, inspiration, and an example of great leadership; the legendary Charlie Allen—if they ever created the position of Commander in Chief/American Intelligence, it would be Charlie; Bert D., legendary and inspirational giant who, to my everlasting good fortune, was my boss and mentor in two tours overseas; Dick J., war hero and a man of such unmatched integrity and good heart that he was affectionately known as "the straight arrow"; Tom T., another legendary professional who hid his steel-trap mind and exceptional leadership behind a Mr. Rogers façade and cardigan sweater; Wick W., Olympic athlete, special-operations veteran, expedition leader, author of several marvelous books, and great friend, with whom my family and I shared many an adventure along the ancient Silk Road; Larry P., another companion on many adventures and an innovator and trailblazer in our Community in the true sense of the word—when they coined the term "sui generis," they had Larry in mind; Pat A., a great friend and leader: we spent many a late night at the office, hammering out some of the principles espoused in this book. He taught me much of what is written down here.

I am also most indebted to CDR Kevin Mullaney, USN, PhD, Director of Leadership Research and his colleagues at the United States Naval Academy; Capt. Wes Huey, USN; Lt. Col. Kyle Phillips, USMC; and Capt. Dan Kokab, USMC, who were kind enough to review the draft and to offer feedback and an invaluable perspective based on their own studies and practical work with the future leaders of the US Navy.

And to the many other brave men and women of the US military and Intelligence Community, particularly in the Program I have been privileged to lead for some years, who put country and mission before self and constantly give me many examples of leadership and patriotic dedication of a level to which I can only aspire.

Made in the USA
Middletown, DE
15 November 2023

42719862R00088